FIND IT
KRUGER NATIONAL PARK

Created by Jacana

Jacana

Published by

Jacana

P O Box 2004, Houghton 2041
Gauteng, South Africa
Tel: (011) 648-1157
Fax: (011) 648-5516
email: marketing@jacana.co.za; www.jacana.co.za

Created and developed by Jacana Education
Illustrations by: Lisl Barry, Joan Beuche, Heather Brooksbank, Glynis Clouston, Pips Kumleben, Sally MacLarty, Michael Thayer, Mike Parkin, Hildegard Windt
Photography by: Malcolm Funston, Paul Funston, Rina Grant, Christo van der Linde, Gary van der Merwe, Kruger Research Department
Digital Scanning: Rainbow Scan / Bureau, Johannesburg
Lithographic Repro: 3 White Dogs, Johannesburg
Printing: Fishwicks the Printers, Durban

The publisher welcomes any comments.
First Edition 1993
Revised and reprinted 1994, 1995
Second Edition 1996
Reprinted 1997
Third Edition 1997
Reprinted 1999
Revised Edition 2000
Reprinted 2001

ISBN 1-919777-70-9

CONTENTS

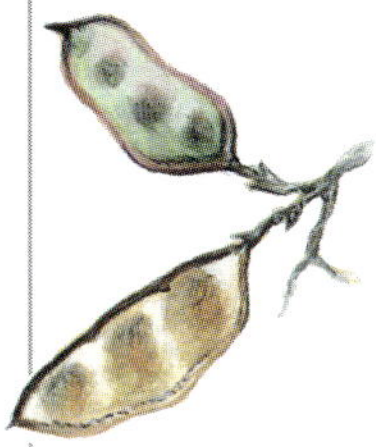
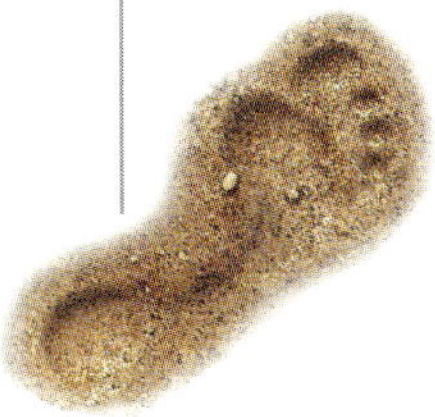

HOW TO USE YOUR GUIDE

The trademark Marula tree, see page 15

1 Study the Ecozone Map or Visitors' Map

These Maps show 16 natural areas (Ecozones) in the Kruger National Park.

- ❑ Each Ecozone has its own combination of geology, land-shape and rainfall.
- ❑ This means that each Ecozone has its own pattern of vegetation and associated animals.
- ❑ Each Ecozone has been given a name, a specific colour and a letter, from **A** to **P** (e.g. **C** – Malelane Mountain Bushveld).

Which Ecozone are you in?

- ❑ Find your place on the Map.
- ❑ Identify the Ecozone that you are in – by colour and letter.
- ❑ Next to the Maps are diagrams with details about each Ecozone.
- ❑ Look for the colour-coded diagram of your Ecozone.

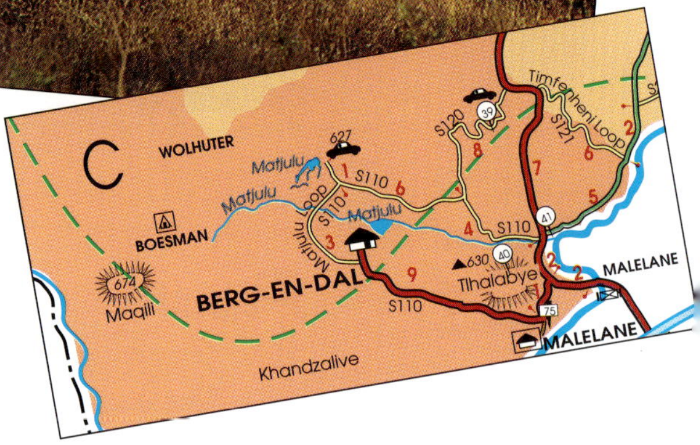

2 Study your Ecozone diagrams on the Maps

- ❑ The diagrams show you the species you can find in your Ecozone – i.e. which trees, grasses and animals are most likely to be seen there e.g. White Rhino and Fever Tree. (Note: The diagrams show where you are most likely to find the species, but do not indicate total distribution.)

RULES
Printed throughout this book, are a few necessary Kruger rules for the safety and protection of the visitors, as well as the animal and plant life. Inconsiderate people who break rules will be fined.

C Malelane Mountain Bushveld (on Granite/Gneiss)

Many unusual plants grow in this mountainous landscape. The plains between the mountains are covered in sweet grass which attracts a variety of grazers.

3 Study the text pages in this book

- ❑ They will give you further, detailed information about the species listed on your Maps, as well as the geology and history of the Kruger National Park.

White Rhino grazing, see page 23

Throughout this book there are

Colour-coded headings

Next to the name of each species is a coloured "corner" like this which ties up with the colour-coded headings. Colour used in this way groups species together which share a common feature.

Note: These colours do not tie up with the Ecozone colours in any way.

4 Create a Mental picture

Look up the species and read all the information. Then you will be able to visualise the animals, birds and plants you are looking for in your Ecozone.

Find the answers to these questions:

- ✦ What do they look like?
- ✦ Where can you find them?
- ✦ What other information will help you find and identify them?

The trunk and branches of the Fever-tree Acacia are a unique yellowish-green, *see page 12*

The following is an example of how to build up a Mental picture

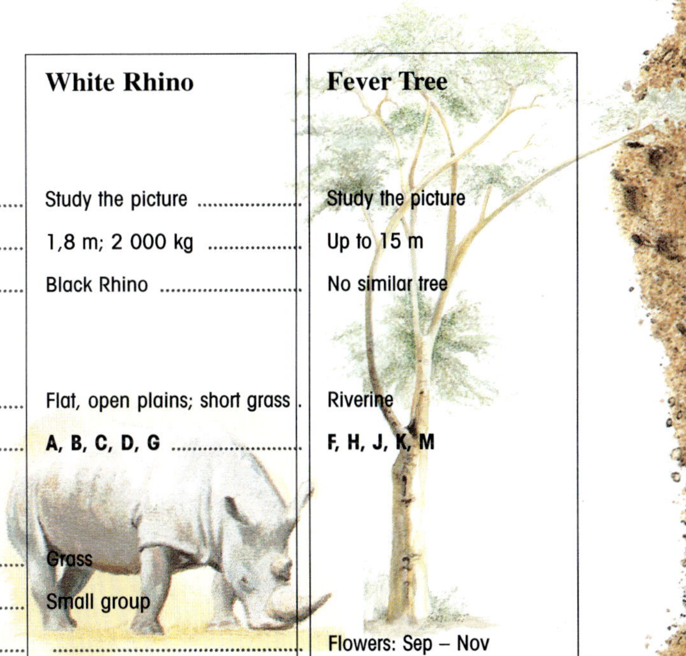

	White Rhino	Fever Tree
What does it look like?		
✦ What shape is it?	Study the picture	Study the picture
✦ What size is it?	1,8 m; 2 000 kg	Up to 15 m
✦ What other species look similar?	Black Rhino	No similar tree
Where do you find it?		
✦ In which habitat?	Flat, open plains; short grass	Riverine
✦ In which Ecozones?	**A, B, C, D, G**	**F, H, J, K, M**
What other information will help you to find it?		
✦ What does it eat?	Grass	
✦ Is it in a family group?	Small group	
✦ Does it have flowers or fruit?		Flowers: Sep – Nov
✦ Does it lose its leaves in winter?		Yes: deciduous

5 Now go out into the bush and find it!

Be sure you are looking for the species in the right Ecozone and right habitat! Keep this book handy and refer to the easy-to-read information regularly.

6 The Ecozone Squares

- ❑ Throughout this book the Ecozone block next to each species represents all 16 Ecozones on the Maps. These Ecozones are identified by the letters **A** – **P**.
- ❑ The individual squares that are **coloured** indicate the Ecozones where you are most likely to find particular species all year round.
- ❑ A few species are difficult to see because they are nocturnal. Their Ecozone blocks are entirely **grey**.
- ❑ Once you have found the species you can circle the relevant coloured Ecozone square.

Rolling Hills south of Skukuza

Rolling Hills north of Punda Maria

Southern Plains – westward from Nkumbe

Shrub Mopane – eastward to Lebombo Mountains

Malelane Mountains – from near Mpondo Dam

Lebombo Mountains

River view – Olifants Get-out Point

Alluvial Plains – Shingwedzi River

GEOLOGY

Everything in Nature is linked

As you spend time in Kruger, read about the way that each element depends on the others.

Plants depend on water and the energy of the sun, as well as food in the soil, for growth. Animals live by eating these plants or eating the flesh of other animals. The waste products of animals feed the soil.

This book will help you to look in the right places, at the right time of the day, to find more, and understand more too.

The species and sites described here are generally common, easy to find and easy to identify. Information about geology of the Lowveld follows on pages 4 - 7.

Do not pick things, damage them or take them away. Try not to change anything.

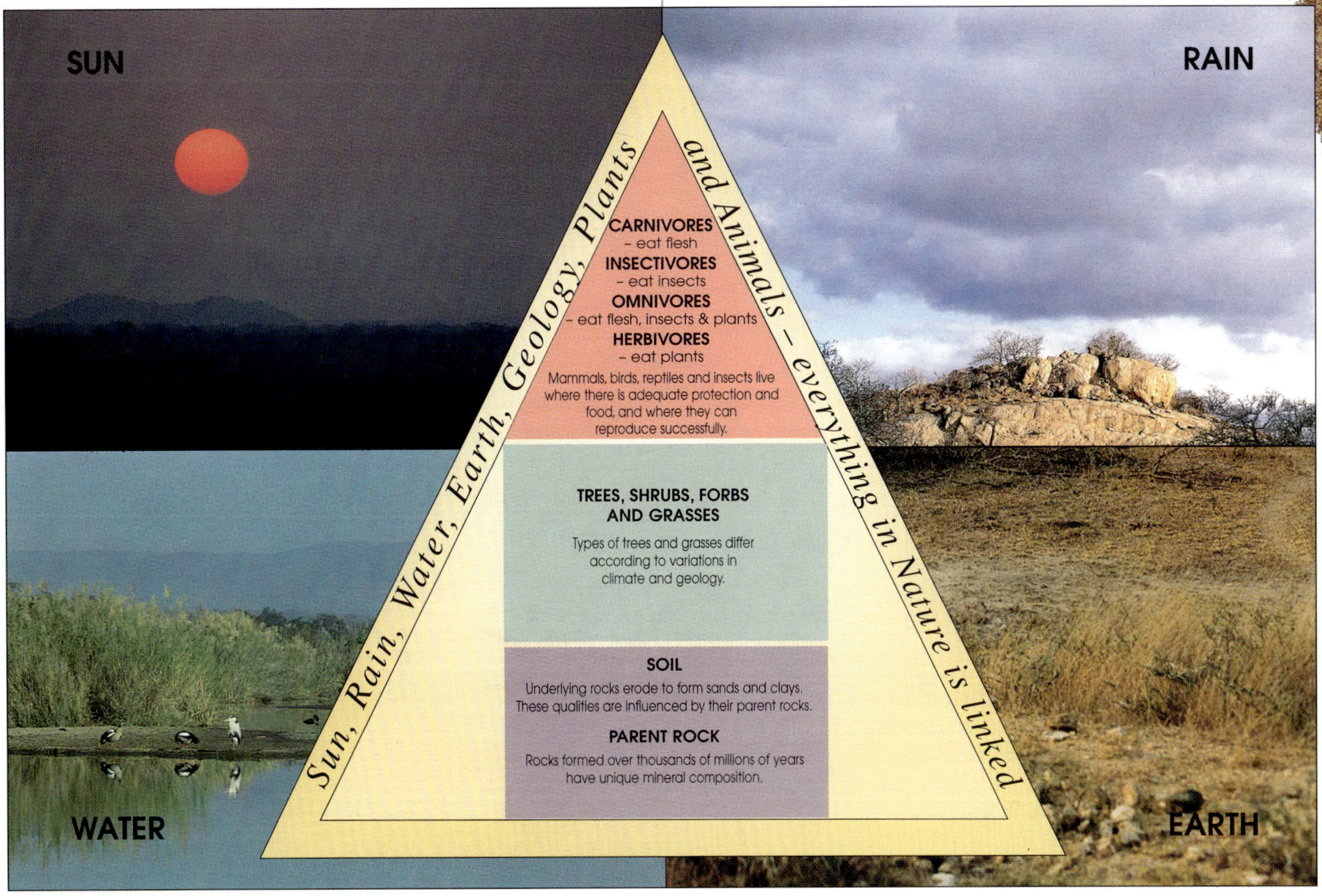

GEOLOGY

How the Lowveld was formed

The Kruger National Park has a fascinating variety of rocks, from some of the oldest known on earth to some of the youngest. And it is all there for you to see.

The earth's surface is changing constantly, but in most cases very slowly.

The rocks below the surface also undergo significant shifts and radical alterations over millions of years.

3 500 – 200 million years ago

The most ancient rocks are older than 3 500 million years. The most common of these are Granite/Gneiss with intrusions of Gabbro.

As a result of a wet, marshy period (about 300 – 200 million years ago), Ecca Shales were laid down on the Granite/Gneiss and Gabbro base.

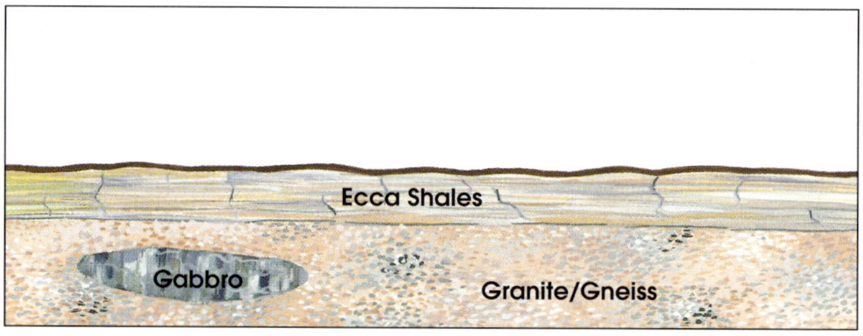

200 – 135 million years ago

The huge primitive Gondwanaland continent started breaking up about 200 million years ago. This break-up was associated with volcanic activity.

Molten rock burst through the crusts of the earth to form layers of Basalt.

Further volcanic activity led to Rhyolite being laid down on top of the Basalt (about 180 million years ago).

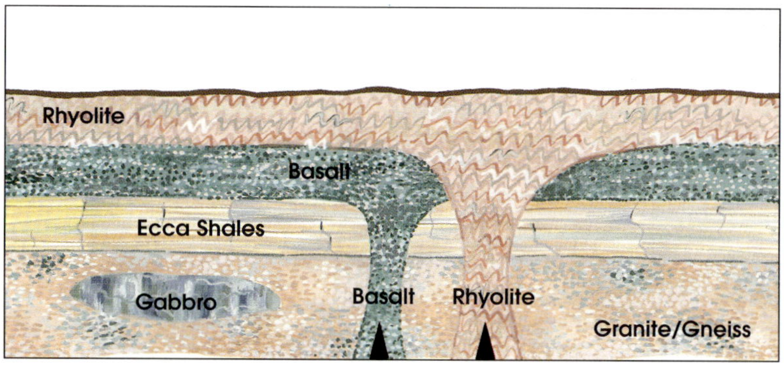

With the breaking up of Gondwanaland, the original flat beds of Granite/Gneiss, Ecca Shales, Basalt and Rhyolite split apart (about 135 million years ago). The eastern half of Southern Africa tilted towards the sea on the east.

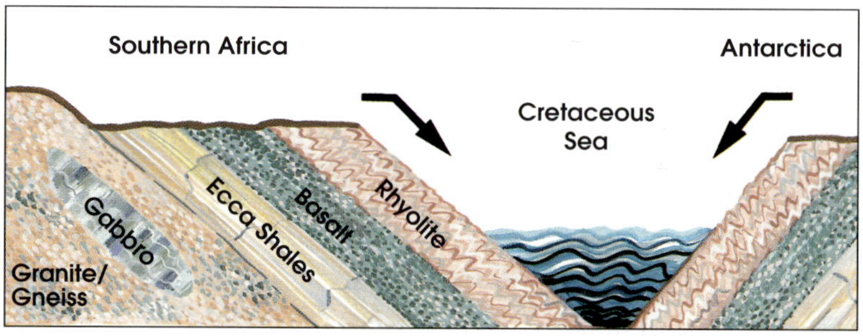

As the new continental edge and coastline of South East Africa developed, many of the present land-shape and ecosystems of the KNP had their beginning.

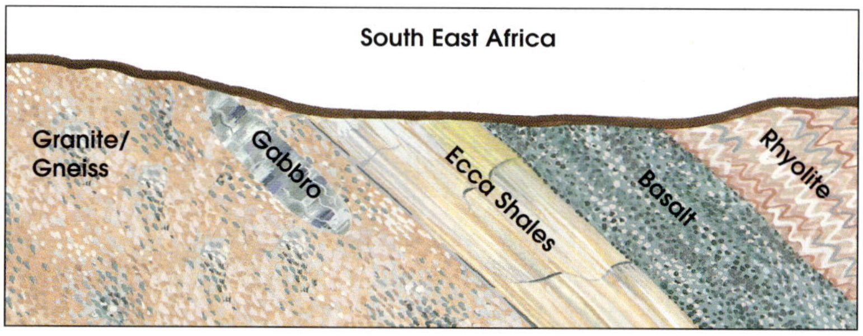

The Lowveld as it is today

The escarpment and Malelane Mountains (in the west) and the Lebombo Mountains (in the east) were the most resistant to the forces of erosion by wind, rain and rivers. They therefore maintained a higher altitude than the rest of the Lowveld.

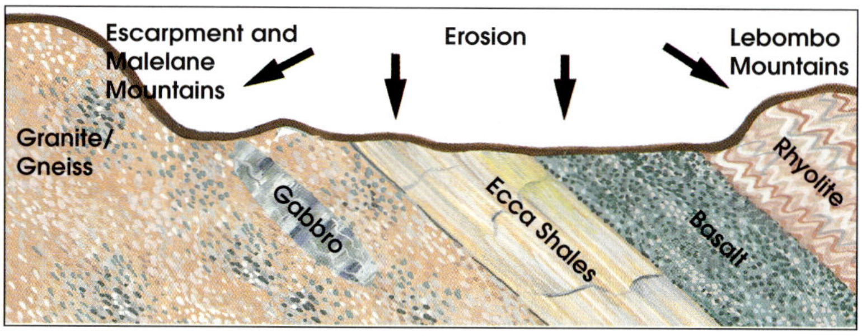

Geological site

The following geological sites are easy to find. They are marked here and on the Kruger National Park ***Map*** with this icon. The shapes, colours and general structure of the rock formations are interesting to look at and could help you to identify the surrounding plants and animals.

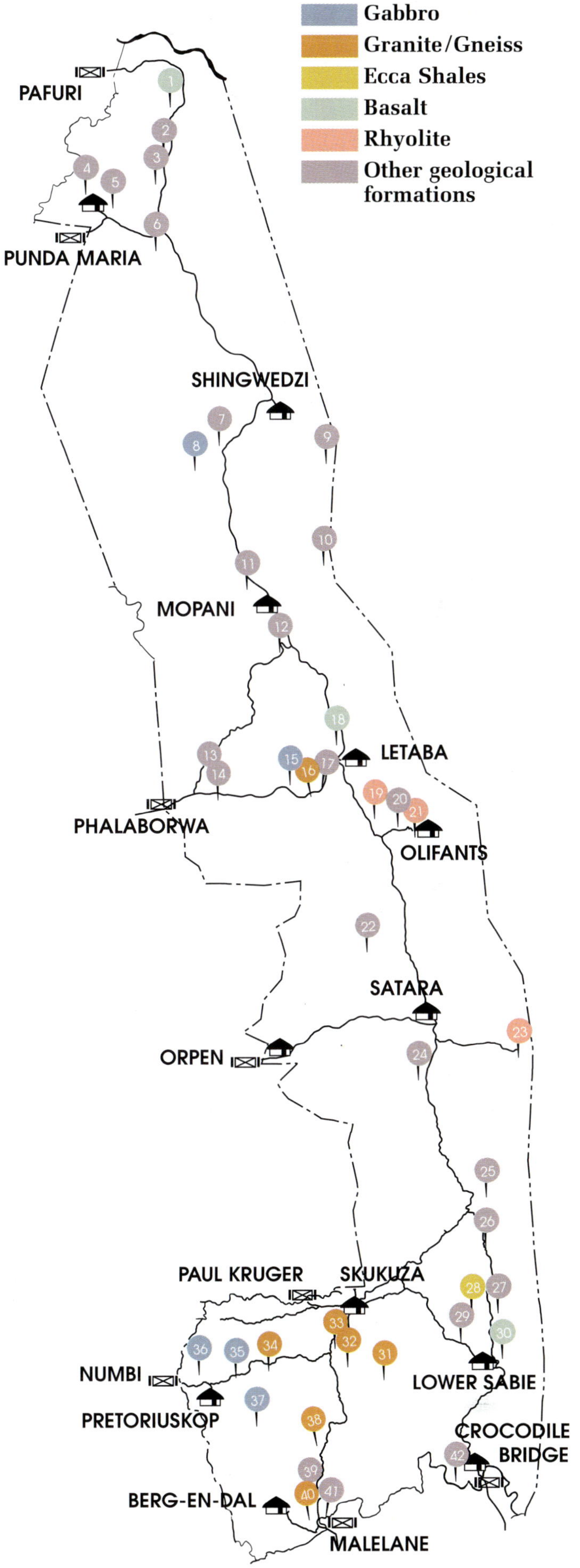

1 Flat-lying, dark-grey flows of **Basalt**

2-3 Light-brown **Clarens Sandstone**, originally formed as massive sand dunes

4-6 Resistant exposures of old, light-brown and red **Soutpansberg Quartzites**

7 Potholed, red **Clarens Sandstone** (Red Rocks)

8 Prominent hills and koppies of columnar, ointed, grey **Gabbro** (Tshanga look-out point)

9 Vertical, grey **Dolerite** dykes

10 Prominent, light-coloured **Granophyre** (ridges at Shibavantsengele)

11 Dark-grey **Nephelinite** rocks, representing ancient volcanic plugs

12 Off-white, coarse **Clarens Sandstone**

13-14 Coarse-grained, orange-coloured **Syenite** plugs (Shikumbu and Masorini)

15 Prominent exposure of blocky, grey **Gabbro**

16 Grey and pink **Granite/Gneiss** cut by light-coloured pegmatite veins

17 Dark-green and black **Greenstone** outcrops

18 Dark-grey **Basalt** flows in river banks and road cuttings (Letaba River and Road S47)

19 Prominent, vertical, light-coloured **Rhyolite** dyke (Shamiriri, extending south to Olifants River)

20 Vertical, grey **Dolerite** dyke

21 Olifants rest camp situated on prominent **Rhyolite** dome

22 Off-white, coarse **Clarens Sandstone** (at picnic-site)

23 Outcrops of reddish **Rhyolite** cut by orange **Granophyre** dykes

24 Off-white, coarse **Clarens Sandstone**

25-27 Prominent, orange-coloured **Granophyre** ridges (N'Wamuriwa, Nkumbe, Muntshe)

28 Bedded, grey **Ecca Shales** and **Mudstone** in river-bank

29 Easterly-dipping, light-coloured **Clarens Sandstone** dune beds (Lubyelubye bridge)

30 Grey **Basalt** flows, cut by **Dolerite** dykes

31-34 Prominent, ancient **Granite/Gneiss** koppies (Grano Kop)

35 Prominent outcrop of blocky, grey **Gabbro**

36 Prominent, ancient **Granite/Gneiss** koppies (Shabeni Kop)

37 Blocky, grey **Gabbro** (Ship Mountain)

38 Ridges and koppies of pink and grey-banded **Granite/Gneiss**

39 Outcrop of dark-coloured **Greenstone**

40 Prominent hillside exposure of dark and light-banded **Granite/Gneiss** (Tlhalabye)

41 Outcrop of dark-coloured **Greenstone**

42 Coarse, light-brown **Clarens Sandstone** outcrops

Remember to refer to your KNP ***Map*** to see which Ecozones have the same underlying geology.

Travel through time

Orpen – N'wanetsi

In the Kruger National Park you can see some fascinating geology, and you can also travel on an adventure through time! In the west, some of the ancient Granite is 3 500 million years old. In the east, the relatively young Basalt and Rhyolite were formed less than 200 million years ago.

Drive along the H7 between Orpen and Satara and along the H6 (or S100) between Satara and N'wanetsi.

As you travel, notice the changes in:

❏ geology ❏ shape of the land ❏ plants ❏ animal distribution

3 500 – 200 million years

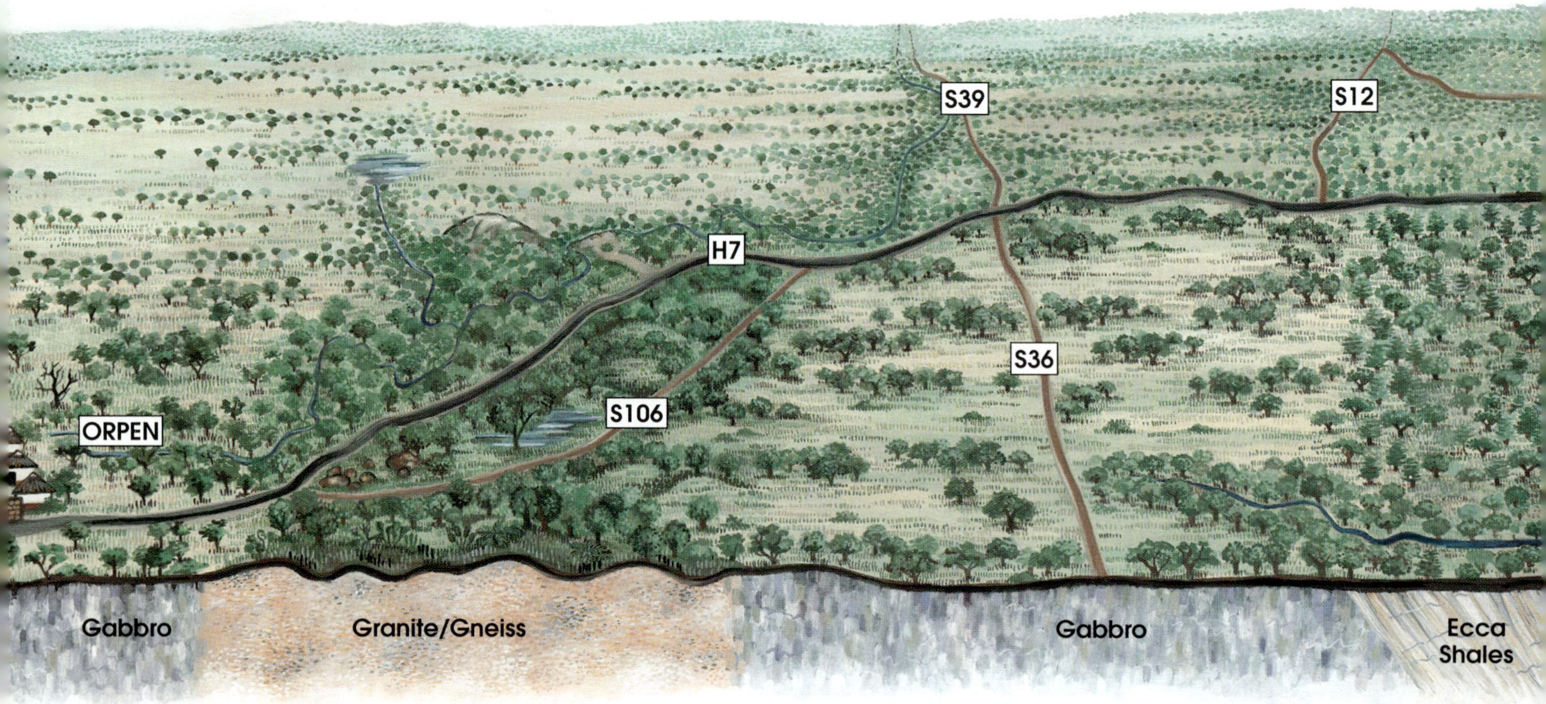

A Mixed Bushwillow Woodlands
(on Granite/Gneiss)

Browsers: Giraffe, Kudu, Impala*, Duiker, Klipspringer, Steenbok
Grazers: Zebra, Buffalo, White rhino, Sable
Predators: Lion, Hyaena, Side-striped jackal
Trees: Bushwillow, Knob thorn
* Browse & graze

E Thorn Veld
(on Gabbro)

Browsers: Giraffe, Kudu, Impala*, Duiker
Grazers: Buffalo, Zebra, Wildebeest, Warthog
Predators: Lion, Hyaena, Cheetah, Black-backed jackal
Trees: Marula, Large knob thorn
*Browse & graze

G

Granite/Gneiss

The underlying Granite/Gneiss gives rise to gently rolling hills and valleys. These are formed by rocks that are more resistant to erosion than the surrounding areas.

Many drainage lines of different sizes (rivers and spruits) can be seen in granite areas. Broad-leaved trees prefer the higher, upland areas while thorn trees prefer lower-lying areas.

Gabbro

These ancient rocks weather to form very fertile soil. This Ecozone has scattered trees and wide open plains, covered by grassland which is very sweet and short, attracting herds of grazers.

Ecca Shales

This area is very flat and water does not penetrate the soils easily. Therefore many pans tend to form.

Remember! Wherever you are in the Kruger, you can use your Map, Ecozone information and the species pages to see more!

Altitude and rainfall

Each Ecozone is an area with its own geology, rainfall, altitude and land-shape.

Look at the rainfall map on the right to see how this relates to some of the Ecozones of the Kruger National Park.

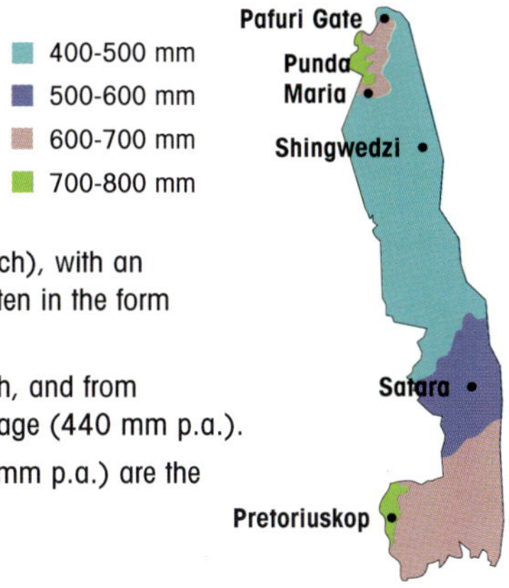

Altitude

The KNP is generally flat to undulating, with the central region averaging 260 m above sea level.

The only higher areas are the Lebombo Mountains in the east, the hills near Punda Maria in the north and the Malelane Mountains in the south. Khandzalive (near Malelane) is the highest point at 839 m above sea level.

Rainfall

The KNP is a summer rainfall area (September to March), with an overall average of 500 mm per annum. The rain is often in the form of thunder-storms.

Rainfall generally decreases from the south to the north, and from the west to the east with Pafuri having the lowest average (440 mm p.a.).

Pretoriuskop (740 mm p.a.) and Punda Maria (600 mm p.a.) are the highest rainfall areas.

200 – 135 million years

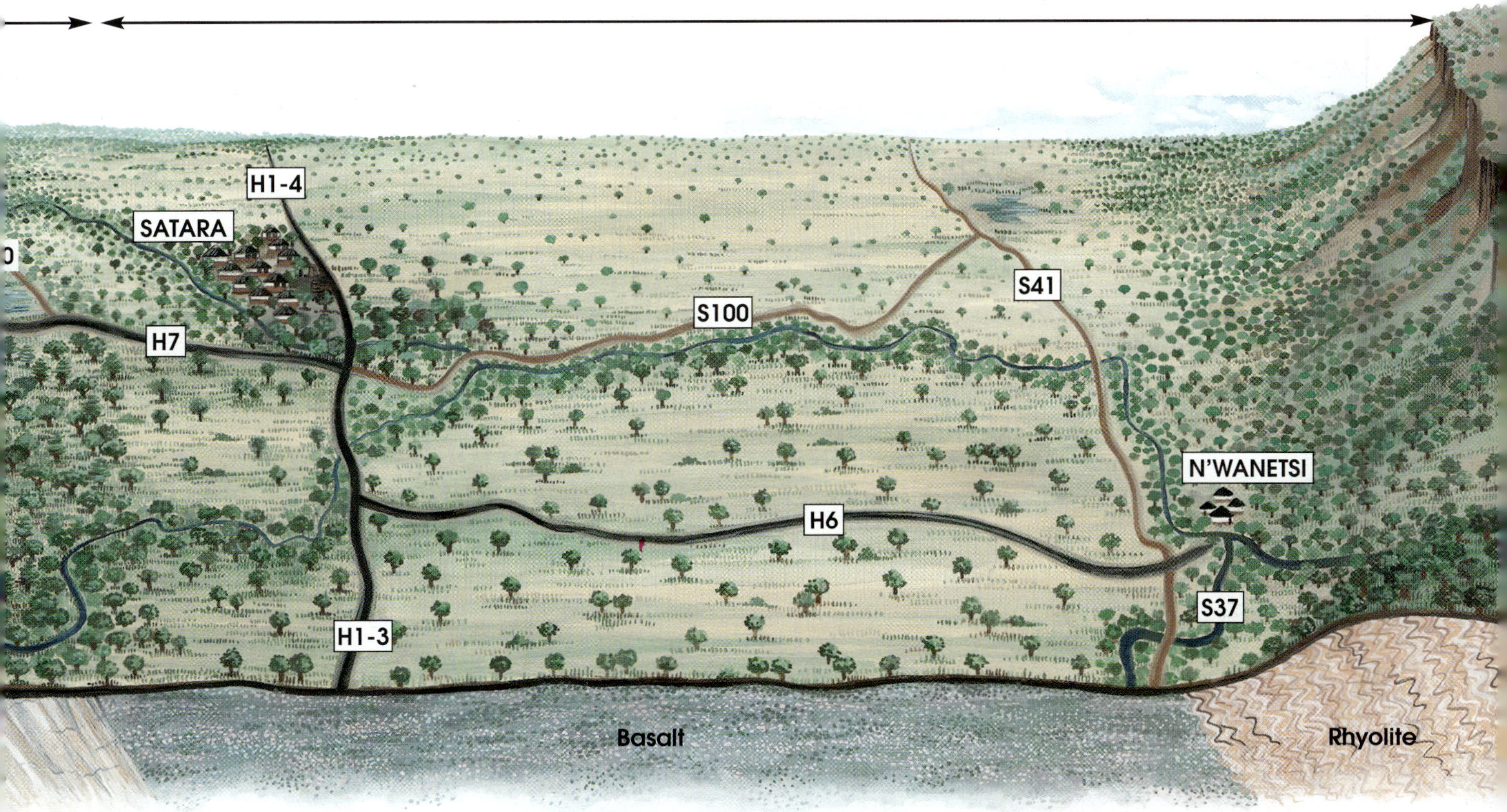

Delagoa Thorn Thickets
(on Ecca Shales)

...owsers: Giraffe, Kudu, Impala*, Duiker, Elephant*, Steenbok
...azers: Zebra, Wildebeest, Buffalo, Waterbuck, White rhino
...edators: Cheetah, Lion, Hyaena, Leopard
...es: Delagoa thorn, Many-stemmed false-thorn
* Browse & graze

There is often abundant game as the grass is very sweet. Patches of open grassveld, often bare through overgrazing, occur between dense thickets of Delagoa thorn trees.

F Knob Thorn/Marula Savannah
(on Basalt)

Browsers: Giraffe, Kudu
Grazers: Zebra, Wildebeest, Buffalo, Tsessebe, Waterbuck, Warthog
Predators: Cheetah, Lion, Hyaena, Black-backed jackal
Trees: Marula, Knob thorn

Basalt

Vast, flat, basalt plains have scattered large trees and shrubs. Soil is clay-based, resulting in few drainage lines and pans of water forming after summer rains.

Vegetation is less variable than in the Granites, but the grass is sweet as a result of the high nutrient value of the clay soil.

I Lebombo Mountain Bushveld
(on Rhyolite)

Browsers: Giraffe, Kudu, Impala*, Klipspringer
Grazers: Zebra, Buffalo, Waterbuck
Predators: Lion
Trees: Comon tree Euphorbia, Baobab (north), Red bushwillow (south)
*Browse & graze

Rhyolite

Rhyolite is more resistant to weathering than Basalt and forms the Lebombo Mountain range. These mountains are rugged with many rocky outcrops and deep ravines. They range over the whole length of Kruger, the north being drier than the south.

Throughout the Kruger you can see examples of the fascinating geological formations. These are listed in detail on page 5.

Buffalo are normally grazers. In times of extreme drought they will also browse.

The following pages describe the grasses and trees that visitors are most likely to see in Kruger.

Watch an elephant carefully as he browses on a shrub or tree. You will see him break off a small branch, roll it in his mouth and eat the bark off the stem.

Bees and many insects pollinate specific plants. Without this interaction these plants would not reproduce and the food source would rapidly die out.

Small antelope, like steenbok and duiker, are generally browsers. They tend to eat forbs which are lower on the ground. Forbs are plants that normally sprout profusely soon after the rain and die back at the end of summer (annuals). They rarely grow as tall as the shrubs and trees that live for many years (perennials).

Zebra prefer to eat grass that is medium-height.

PLANTS

There are thousands of varieties of plants in the Kruger National Park. They are fascinating in their own right – but are also of great interest because of the never-ending cycle of interaction between plant and animal worlds.

All plants (whether grasses or others) vary in their attraction as food depending on:

- how tasty they are
- how high the actual food value is

There are two types of plants which offer food to animals:

- **Grasses**
- **Non-grasses –** trees, shrubs, climbers and forbs

You will find different animals in different areas of the Kruger, according to the food they eat.

Animals that eat plants are called herbivores. Herbivores can generally be divided into two groups:

- **Grazers** that mostly eat grasses
- **Browsers** that mostly eat non-grasses

A few animals, like impala and elephant, graze **and** browse. Their choice will depend on which plants offer the best quality food in an area.

Different grazers eat different types of grass in the varying seasons. However, they do have a preference about the height of the grass they graze. Roan and sable feed off taller grasses. Wildebeest prefer very short grasses, and therefore often follow zebra that graze medium-height grasses. Grass savannah provides food for a large number of animals. Therefore grazers are often herd animals.

Wooded, bushy areas cannot feed as many animals as the same size grassland. Browsers therefore tend to be solitary or in small groups.

Termites carry dry grasses and leaves below the surface of the ground into the termitaria (anthills/termite mounds). This fertilises and aerates the soil. The recycling of plant material is essential to ensure that the food taken out of the soil by vegetation is returned for future growth.

Kudu are amongst the larger browsers. Different browsers eat at different heights and from different types of plants. Browsers generally obtain food from softer leaves, bark, flowers and pods.

Buffalo prefer tall, coarse grass

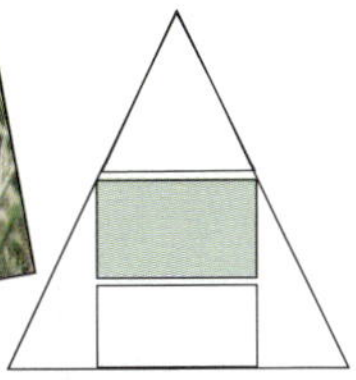

TREES, SHRUBS, FORBS AND GRASSES

Grasses and reeds

The kind of grazer you are likely to see partly depends on the state and the species of grass in that area.

Animals choose to graze a specific grass depending on its palatability (taste).

Species of grass have different levels of taste and food value, depending on:

- ❑ type of grass
- ❑ soil where it grows
- ❑ amount of rainfall in the area
- ❑ amount of rainfall that season
- ❑ age of the specific plant
  (some grasses are only palatable and nutritious while they are young)

You should see more grazers where grass is palatable and nutritious.

"Mixed grass" on the Maps refers to an area where both "sweet" and "sour" grass grows.

Areas where grass tends to be palatable and nutritious throughout the year are called "sweet" grassveld areas.

Where grass grows fast and tall, rainfall is normally high. This grass usually become fibrous and unpalatable when it matures. These areas are known as "Sourveld" areas, such as in Ecozone B (Pretoriuskop Sourveld).

Further reading:
Guide to Grasses of South Africa
– Frits van Oudtshoorn

Grasses – Group A

These grasses are generally palatable and nutritious – "sweet" grasses – eaten by most grazers. These species decrease with over-utilization.

Blue Buffalo Grass
Cenchrus ciliaris
Up to 1 m; perennial
Habitat: Occurs on most soils; on termitaria
Seed: Aug – Apr
Utilization: Very palatable when young

A	E	I	M
B	F	J	N
C	G	K	O
D	H	L	P

Finger Grass
Digitaria eriantha
Up to 1,4 m; perennial
Habitat: Open areas on most soils, especially sandy areas
Seed: Jan – Apr
Utilization: Extensive

A	E	I	M
B	F	J	N
C	G	K	O
D	H	L	P

Guinea Grass
Panicum maximum
Up to 2,5 m; perennial
Habitat: All soils; damp places with fertile soil; shade of trees; along rivers
Seed: Nov – Jul
Utilization: Extensive, particularly white rhino

A	E	I	M
B	F	J	N
C	G	K	O
D	H	L	P

Vlei Bristle Grass
Setaria incrassata
Up to 2 m; perennial
Habitat: Basalt; Gabbro; heavy, clay soils; vleis & marshes
Seed: Oct – May
Utilization: Most grazers

A	E	I	M
B	F	J	N
C	G	K	O
D	H	L	P

Rooigras (Red Grass)
Themeda triandra
0,3-1,5 m; perennial
Habitat: Basalt; Gabbro; Dolerite; undisturbed grassland areas
Seed: Oct – Jul
Utilization: Tall-grass grazers, like buffalo

A	E	I	M
B	F	J	N
C	G	K	O
D	H	L	P

Grass is usually easy to identify by its seed-head (inflorescence). Most seed-heads develop during the summer months (September to April).

Reeds – Group B

Reeds provide dry season grazing.

Reeds
Phragmites australis
Up to 4 m; perennial
Habitat: Near water; often form dense stands
Seed: Dec – Jun
Utilization: Buffalo, hippo & elephant, for dry season grazing

A	E	I	M
B	F	J	N
C	G	K	O
D	H	L	P

Grasses – Group C

These grasses are generally not palatable or nutritious and are only eaten when young and tender.

These species increase with over-utilization.

A	E	I	M
B	F	J	N
C	G	K	O
D	H	L	P

Spear Grass
Heteropogon contortus

Up to 0,7 m; perennial; fast-growing grass
Habitat: Well-drained stony soils; open areas; twisted seed-heads are often seen along roadsides
Seed: Oct – Jun
Utilization: Roan & waterbuck

Stinking Grass
Bothriochloa radicans

Up to 0,7 m
Habitat: Drier Basalt areas; heavy, clay soil; around termite mounds; stony slopes
Seed: Oct – Apr
Utilization: Only when young

A	E	I	M
B	F	J	N
C	G	K	O
D	H	L	P

Nine-awned Grass
Enneapogon cenchroides

Up to 1 m; hardy grass that withstands drought
Habitat: Sandy, soils; disturbed areas
Seed: Dec – May
Utilization: Fairly well when young

A	E	I	M
B	F	J	N
C	G	K	O
D	H	L	P

Cat's Tail
Perotis patens

Up to 0,6 m
Habitat: Poor, sandy soils; dry, bare patches; disturbed areas
Seed: Nov – Apr

A	E	I	M
B	F	J	N
C	G	K	O
D	H	L	P

Broad-leaved Curly Leaf
Eragrostis rigidior

Up to 1 m; perennial
Habitat: Sandy, loam soils; open areas; disturbed soils
Seed: Oct – May

A	E	I	M
B	F	J	N
C	G	K	O
D	H	L	P

Grasses – Group D

These grasses are nutritious but only palatable when young – "sour" grasses.

These species increase with under-utilization.

Fine Thatching Grass
Hyparrhenia filipendula

Up to 1,5 m; perennial
Habitat: All soils; high rainfall; near vleis & rivers
Seed: Nov – Apr
Utilization: Tall-grass feeders

A	E	I	M
B	F	J	N
C	G	K	O
D	H	L	P

Yellow Thatching Grass
Hyperthelia dissoluta

Up to 3 m; very woody & tall; perennial
Habitat: Granitic, sandy soils; open areas; higher rainfall; disturbed soils
Seed: Jan – Jun
Utilization: Tall-grass feeders

A	E	I	M
B	F	J	N
C	G	K	O
D	H	L	P

Creeping Bristle Grass
Setaria sphacelata

Up to 0,5 m
Habitat: Granitic, well-drained soils; important in soil conservation as it forms runners which bind the soil
Seed: Sep – Mar

A	E	I	M
B	F	J	N
C	G	K	O
D	H	L	P

Utilization by animals refers to grazing.

Trees

This list covers some of the more important, common trees and shrubs in the Kruger National Park, as well as those which are easy for you to find. It is not, however, a complete tree list by which you can identify every tree in the KNP. If you have difficulty in recognising trees, read *Sappi Tree Spotting – Lowveld*.

Use these pages to identify common trees and shrubs easily.

- From your ***Map*** work out in which Ecozone you are.
- Read the diagram for your specific Ecozone to understand which trees can be found in the different habitats (e.g. on hill crests, valley bottoms etc.)
- Look up these trees on th following pages**.** The pictures and the comments will help you to form a mental picture of each tree.
- *Now try to find that specific tree, in that specific habitat... in the KNP!*

All trees listed below have a national tree number. These are the same as the numbers on some trees in the KNP. All deciduous trees are illustrated with summer foliage on the left side & bare winter branches on the right.

Further reading:
Sappi Tree Spotting Lowveld – Jacana

Tree groups that are easy to recognise

Thorn trees (Acacias)

There are many different Acacias; some are easy to recognise. All Acacias have compound leaves, which are favoured by browsers & heavily thorned for protection against browsing. Tree shape, pod & thorn shape can help you to identify them.

This illustration represents the two Acacias described below.

168.1
Horned-thorn Acacia
Acacia grandicornuta
9 m; deciduous
Thorns: Long (8 cm), straight, white (hard, sharp); in pairs
Flowers: Oct – Feb
Fruit: Mar – Sep
Utilization: Browsed; pods utilized by baboons & monkeys

A	E	I	M
B	F	J	N
C	G	K	O
D	H	L	P

179
Scented-pod Acacia
Acacia nilotica, subsp. *kraussiana*
Up to 7 m; deciduous
Trunk: Short, bare, crooked; divides low
Crown: Spreading round; branches hang downwards
Thorns: Long, slender, straight, white; in pairs
Flowers: Oct – Feb; round, bright-yellow, fragrant groups
Fruit: Mar – Sep; green-black; sticky; sweet-smelling, segmented
Utilization: Important browsing for smaller antelope

A	E	I	M
B	F	J	N
C	G	K	O
D	H	L	P

A	E	I	M
B	F	J	N
C	G	K	O
D	H	L	P

189
Fever-tree Acacia
Acacia xanthophloea
Up to 15 m; deciduous
Trunk: Slender, bare, fairly high-branching
Bark: Unique, yellowy-green
Thorns: Long, white, slender; in pairs
Flowers: Aug – Sep; bright-yellow, dense, small balls
Fruit: Late summer; highly utilized
Utilization: Leaves, branches & gum extensively; often damaged by elephants

163
Delagoa Acacia
Acacia welwitschii, subsp. *delagoensis*
Up to 15 m; deciduous
Trunk: Usually straight, high-branching but with many lateral twigs making low-down, untidy bush
Crown: Spreading; fairly dense, untidy appearance
Thorns: Paired, hooked, small, grey-black
Flowers: Nov – Jan; white, spikes in clusters
Fruit: May – Jul
Utilization: Important food plant for many browsers

A	E	I	M
B	F	J	N
C	G	K	O
D	H	L	P

183.1
Narrow-pod Splendid Acacia (Brack Thorn)
Acacia robusta, subsp. *clavigera*
Up to 20 m; deciduous
Trunk: Single; high-branching; branches stretch upwards
Bark: Dark-grey to black; rough, fissured
Crown: Very dense, very dark-green; conspicuous along major rivers for dark, tidy, upward -reaching appearance
Thorns: Long, straight, white; in pairs
Flowers: Late winter – early spring; small, light yellow-white, sweet-scented
Fruit: Late summer; almost sickle-shaped; burst open while on the tree; seeds fall much later
Utilization: Sometimes browsed by elephants & kudu

A	E	I	M
B	F	J	N
C	G	K	O
D	H	L	P

PIPS KUHNLEBEN

Thorn trees (Acacias)

188
Umbrella Acacia
Acacia tortilis, subsp. *heteracantha*

Up to 11 m; deciduous
Trunk: Short, branches out laterally to form umbrella shape
Thorns: Two kinds on each tree: small, brown, hooked; long, straight, white
Flowers: Nov – Dec; many white, round heads
Fruit: May – Jun
Utilization: Heavily browsed by all browsers
• Very easy to find

A	E	I	M
B	F	J	N
C	G	K	O
D	H	L	P

A	E	I	M
B	F	J	N
C	G	K	O
D	H	L	P

178
Knob-thorn Acacia
Acacia nigrescens

Up to 16 m; deciduous
Bark: Dark, grooved, rough
Leaves: Lacy, small, pale-green
Thorns: Knobs mainly grow on lower & younger branches, each tipped with a small, black, hooked thorn; initially thorns occur in pairs on branchlets
Flowers: Jun – Sep; many, small, white spikes
Fruit: Oct – Jan
Utilization: Heavily browsed, particularly by giraffe

False-thorn trees (Albizias)

Leaves are compound and often confused with Acacias; thornless.

154
Broad-pod Albizia
Albizia forbesii

Up to 10 m; deciduous
Habitat: Usually along rivers
Trunk: Single, straight, mostly bare
Flowers: Oct – Nov; fairly large, fragile, puff-like, white; long stamens
Fruit: Late summer; dark-brown, twisted, ridged
Utilization: Browsed

A	E	I	M
B	F	J	N
C	G	K	O
D	H	L	P

A	E	I	M
B	F	J	N
C	G	K	O
D	H	L	P

153
Many-stemmed Albizia
Albizia petersiana, subsp. *evansii*

Up to 11 m; deciduous
Habitat: Grow together with Delagoa thorn (**163**) on sandy soils on Ecca Shales
Trunk: Multi-stemmed; spreading rapidly to form distinctive V-shape
Crown: Wide
Flowers: Dec; small heads; petals small, white; stamens fused to form blood-red tube
Fruit: Summer – autumn
Utilization: Leaves browsed

Euphorbias

The Euphorbias have characteristic succulent-like thick, green branches, like chubby fingers.

346
Deadliest Candelabra Euphorbia (Bushveld Candelabra Euphorbia)
Euphorbia cooperi

Up to 7 m
Trunk: Long, single, bare; branches arise from the trunk at a common point; lower branches die off annually, leaving holes in stem; latex extremely poisonous
Flowers: May – Aug; yellow-green
Fruit: Aug – Oct
Utilization: Not browsed; fruit eaten by seed-eating birds
• Very easy to find

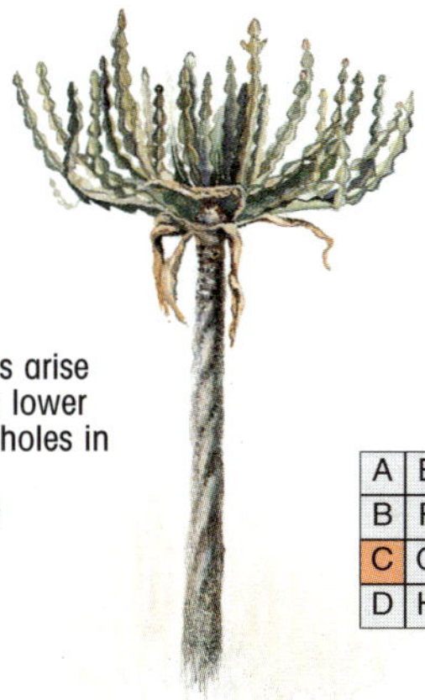

A	E	I	M
B	F	J	N
C	G	K	O
D	H	L	P

A	E	I	M
B	F	J	N
C	G	K	O
D	H	L	P

351
Naboom (Common Tree Euphorbia)
Euphorbia ingens

Up to 15 m
Habitat: On hills; rocky outcrops
Trunk: Short; branches do not die off, but multiply & divide; leafless; latex very poisonous
Flowers: Spring – winter; small yellowy-green
Fruit: Spring; green, roughly round
Utilization: Not browsed; fruit eaten by seed-eating birds
• Very easy to find

NOTE:

Many of these trees occur in a number of different Ecozones and in different habitats that are not mentioned here.

There they may grow differently and may be difficult to recognise from these descriptions.

This list is designed to introduce you to easily recognisable trees in their common habitats.

"Utilization" refers to the extent leaves and bark are eaten by browsers.

Bushwillows (Combretums)

Four common species of Combretum occur, three of which are similar.

Common features of Bushwillows

- ❑ Either low-branching with shortish, crooked stem; or no main trunk with multi-stem, having smaller branchlets growing up from the base
- ❑ Dense stands can cover large areas
- ❑ Usually deciduous
- ❑ Fruits four-winged
- ❑ No thorns

A	E	I	M
B	F	J	N
C	G	K	O
D	H	L	P

546
Large-fruit Bushwillow
Combretum zeyheri

Up to 12 m; deciduous
Habitat: Granite & Rhyolite
Leaves: 8,5 x 4 cm
Fruit: Up to 6 cm diameter

Main differences between Bushwillows

- ❑ Size
- ❑ Habitat
- ❑ Size of leaves
- ❑ Size of fruits

538
Russet Bushwillow
Combretum hereroense

A	E	I	M
B	F	J	N
C	G	K	O
D	H	L	P

Up to 8 m; deciduous
Habitat: Along rivers & streams; low-lying, rocky areas
Leaves: 3 x 2 cm
Flowers: Aug – Oct
Fruit: Midsummer; 2,3 x 2 cm; russet-brown colour

A	E	I	M
B	F	J	N
C	G	K	O
D	H	L	P

532
Red Bushwillow
Combretum apiculatum, subsp. *apiculatum*

Up to 9 m; deciduous
Habitat: Granitic & rhyolitic soils; rocky areas
Leaves: 6,5 x 3,5 cm
Flowers: Aug – Nov
Fruit: Summer – autumn; 2,5 x 2 cm

The Bushwillow illustrated here represents the three Bushwillows described above (532, 546, 538)

A	E	I	M
B	F	J	N
C	G	K	O
D	H	L	P

539
Leadwood
Combretum imberbe

Up to 20 m; deciduous
Habitat: Found everywhere in association with Knob thorn **(178)** and Marula **(360)**
Trunk: Single, thick, bare; extremely hard wood
Bark: Pale-grey, small, irregular, brick pattern
Crown: Old dead branchlets & branches do not break off easily; rather sparse foliage & small leaf for tree of this size
Flowers: Nov – Dec; small, yellow-green
Fruit: Autumn; small, brown-winged seeds
Utilization: Browsers

Palms

These appear in tree or shrub form.

Shapes are very distinctive with huge, spiky leaves.

Leaves are in clusters in shrubs, and at top of trunk in tree forms.

22
Wild Date-palm
Phoenix reclinata

Up to ± 6 m; evergreen
Habitat: Always found near water, on river banks & vleis
Trunk: Remnants of old leaves on trunk
Leaves: Arching with leaflets growing from central spine
Fruit: Date-like; yellow
Utilization: Browsed by elephant; birds, baboons & monkeys eat the fruit
• Very easy to find

A	E	I	M
B	F	J	N
C	G	K	O
D	H	L	P

23
Southern Lala-palm
Hyphaene natalensis

Up to 15 m; evergreen
Habitat: Not necessarily near water; clay soil
Trunk: Suckers from base grow in clumps
Leaves: Fan-like from central point
Fruit: Large (6 cm); hard, dark-brown, shiny
Utilization: Browsed by elephant
• Very easy to find

A	E	I	M
B	F	J	N
C	G	K	O
D	H	L	P

"Utilization" refers to the extent leaves and bark are eaten by browsers.

Trees that are easy to recognise by their shape

The following trees are easy to identify because they each have special bark, shape, colour or leaf formation.
Often a combination of some of these features will help you to build up a mental picture of the tree you are looking for.
Now try to find the tree in Kruger.

Clay soil

222
Tree Wistaria
Bolusanthus speciosus

Up to 15 m, deciduous
Trunk: Slender, single or forked; few branches
Bark: Brown; deeply fissured
Crown: Whole tree drooping, soft, delicate appearance
Leaves: Long, light-green, glossy, drooping; 11-13 leaflets
Flowers: Sept – Oct; violet-blue drooping grape-like bunches
Fruit: Feb – Mar; brown to black
Utilization: Browsed

A	E	I	M
B	F	J	N
C	G	K	O
D	H	L	P

238
Apple-leaf (Rain Tree)
Lonchocarpus capassa

Up to 18 m (Riverine, Alluvial); elsewhere up to 10 m; deciduous (leaves fall in spring); "Rain tree" name from fluid dripped by froth-covered insects feeding on tree in early summer
Trunk: Twisted
Crown: Branches wide-spreading; bare; sometimes carry separated clumps of crown
Leaves: Large; look faded
Flowers: Late summer; pale mauve, dense, drooping clusters
Fruit: Oct – Jan; green to pale-brown clusters; remain on trees
Utilization: Browsed by elephants in dry periods
• ***Very easy to find***

A	E	I	M
B	F	J	N
C	G	K	O
D	H	L	P

A	E	I	M
B	F	J	N
C	G	K	O
D	H	L	P

360
Marula
Sclerocarya birrea, subsp. *caffra*

Up to 15 m; deciduous
Trunk: Straight, long, bare, high-branching
Bark: Flakes off irregularly, showing yellow-pink blocks
Crown: Wide-spread, round, fairly dense; branchlets finger-like, end abruptly
Flowers: Aug – Sep; mixed, dark red-pink-white; separate (M) & (F) trees
Fruit: Jan – Feb; green berries; ripen yellow
Utilization: Highly favoured by all species; heavily browsed

Sandy soil

A	E	I	M
B	F	J	N
C	G	K	O
D	H	L	P

551
Silver Cluster-leaf
Terminalia sericea

Smallish; 8 m; deciduous
Habitat: Found in groups/lines at the seepline, half way down a slope
Trunk: Single, slender, low-branching
Bark: Grey; vertically ridged
Crown: Branches lateral, growing at right angles to the trunk, (resembles a waiter carrying a tray)
Leaves: In clusters, giving silvery impression
Flowers: Oct – Nov; dirty-white small spikes; strong smelling
Fruit: Mar – Apr; buff-green, then pinkish
Utilization: Seldom browsed; fruit eaten by insects

A	E	I	M
B	F	J	N
C	G	K	O
D	H	L	P

251
Y-thorned Torchwood (Green Thorn)
Balanites maughamii

Up to 20 m; semi-deciduous
Trunk: Fluted, as if many trunks have been joined together; tall, straight, usually branching high up; some side shoots often low down
Leaves: Look rigid, quite brittle; consist of twin leaflets
Thorns: Forked, green
Fruit: May – Jul; like dates; mature yellow-brown
Utilization: Regularly browsed; particularly by elephant & giraffe; fruit eaten by impala & baboon
• ***Very easy to find***

Trees that are easy to recognise in specific habitats

The following trees are easy to identify because each one is common in a specific habitat. Look at the pictures and read the descriptions, which will help you to build up a mental picture of the tree. Now try to find the tree in the Park!

Near permanent water

341
Tamboti
Spirostachys africana

Up to 10 m; deciduous, leaves turn red-brown
Bark: Divided into small rectangles in rows like rough snake-skin
Crown: Quite dense; very poisonous latex in leaves, & even smoke from braai causes nausea
Flowers: Aug – Sep
Fruit: Sep – Oct; insects (pupae) cause fruit to "hop" on ground
Utilization: Bark & leaves utilized by black rhino & porcupine

A	E	I	M
B	F	J	N
C	G	K	O
D	H	L	P

A	E	I	M
B	F	J	N
C	G	K	O
D	H	L	P

66
Sycomore Fig (Common Cluster Fig)
Ficus sycomorus, subsp. *sycomorus*

Up to 20 m; mostly evergreen; enormous and spreading
Trunk: Huge, thick & short-fluted that often has low-down thick, spreading branches
Bark: Very noticeable, yellowish, skin-like
Fruit: All year; very visible
Utilization: Seldom browsed; fruit eaten by birds & animals
• Very easy to find

A	E	I	M
B	F	J	N
C	G	K	O
D	H	L	P

684
Matumi
Breonadia salicina

Up to 40 m; evergreen; smaller ones are easy to recognise
Leaves: Long, fairly thick, dark-green, glossy; grow in groups of four
Flowers: Nov – Mar; very small, pale-yellow, densely packed in round heads
Fruit: Jan – Feb; extremely small; inconspicuous
Utilization: Not browsed
• Very easy to find

A	E	I	M
B	F	J	N
C	G	K	O
D	H	L	P

301
Woodland Trichilia (Natal Mahogany)
Trichilia emetica

Up to 20 m; evergreen
Trunk: Thick & dark; low-branching
Crown: Very dense; round
Leaves: Big, shiny, dark-green
Flowers: Aug – Sep; green, dense clusters
Fruit: Drooping clusters
Utilization: Seldom browsed; fruit eaten by birds

678
Sausage-tree
Kigelia africana

Up to 20 m; semi-deciduous to deciduous
Trunk: Very thick, short, straight
Crown: Wide-spreading, dense, round
Leaves: Shed late winter – early spring
Flowers: Jul – Oct; distinctive
Fruit: Appear after Aug, drop Mar – Apr; sausages distinctive; not eaten
Utilization: Seldom browsed

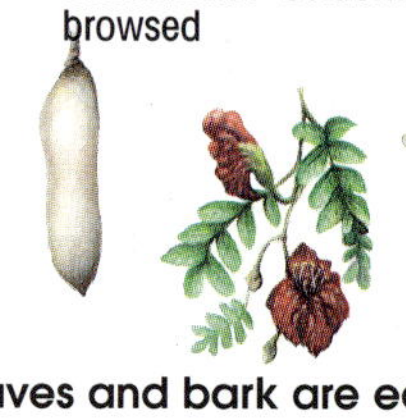

A	E	I	M
B	F	J	N
C	G	K	O
D	H	L	P

"Utilization" refers to the extent leaves and bark are eaten by browsers.

Often on termitaria (anthills)

606
Ebony Jackal-berry (African Ebony)
Diospyros mespiliformis

Up to 20 m; deciduous; distinguishing feature is often size
Habitat: Riverine; sometimes on termitaria
Trunk: Single; divides into branches that appear almost as thick as trunk
Bark: Dark, almost black; can be confused with Tamboti **(341)**
Leaves: Dark-green; autumn dark-yellow
Fruit: Sep – Oct
Utilization: Seldom browsed; fruit eaten by birds & other animals (especially primates)

A	E	I	M
B	F	J	N
C	G	K	O
D	H	L	P

202
Weeping Boer-bean
Schotia brachypetala

Up to 12 m; deciduous
Bark : Rough, dark-grey; peels in small irregular blocks
Crown: Similar to Sausage tree **(678)** with smaller leaves that appear to grow downwards; branches rigid, like fingers pointing downwards, giving quite dense umbrella shape
Flowers: Early spring; distinctive red
Fruit: Late summer; from pale-green to dark-brown; pale-yellow attachments to seeds
Utilization: Seldom browsed; young shoots only; pods eaten by birds

A	E	I	M
B	F	J	N
C	G	K	O
D	H	L	P

On rocky outcrops

A	E	I	M
B	F	J	N
C	G	K	O
D	H	L	P

63
Large-leaved Rock Fig
Ficus abutilifolia

Up to 6 m; deciduous; distinctive, beautiful, branching, white roots that seem to hold rocks with long "syrupy" fingers
Trunk: Short, twisting, yellow-white
Fruit: All year; quite large, red when ripe
Utilization: Not browsed; fruit eaten by birds, primates & other game
• Very easy to find

A	E	I	M
B	F	J	N
C	G	K	O
D	H	L	P

269
Mountain Kirkia (Mountain Seringa)
Kirkia wilmsii

Illustration as for White Seringa **(267)** below, except trunk multi-stemmed & low-branching
Up to 10 m; deciduous
Crown: Roundish
Leaves: Same as White seringa
Flowers: Sep – Oct; masses of small yellow-green clusters
Fruit: Feb – Mar
Utilization: Limited, except by elephants

A	E	I	M
B	F	J	N
C	G	K	O
D	H	L	P

267
White Kirkia (White Seringa)
Kirkia acuminata

Up to 20 m; deciduous
Trunk: Long, straight, bare; thicker, older branches also bare
Crown: Spreads flat, silhouettes against the sky, on top of koppies
Leaves: Look like feather-dusters, crowded at the branch ends
Flowers: Oct – Dec; white clusters on long stalks
Fruit: Apr – May; visible through winter
Utilization: Browsed occasionally

Trees that are easy to recognise in specific habitats (continued)

More common in the north

207
Pod-mahogany
Afzelia quansensis

Up to 20 m; deciduous
Trunk: Single, straight; sometimes huge
Bark: Pale grey-creamy brown, smoothish with circular ridges
Crown: Dense, spreading, sometimes wider than tree height
Leaves: Compound; leaflets shiny, waxy, feathery, wavy, drooping
Flowers: Oct – Nov; green, red-spotted, single petal
Fruit: Nov – Jan; most beautiful when open, showing white lining & red & black seeds
Utilization: Browsed by elephants

A	E	I	M
B	F	J	N
C	G	K	O
D	H	L	P

A	E	I	M
B	F	J	N
C	G	K	O
D	H	L	P

241
Nyala-tree
Xanthocercis zambesiaca

Up to 30 m; evergreen to semi-deciduous
Trunk: Single, fluted; low-branching
Crown: Dense, spreading, rounded; spread often wider than height; branches drooping at ends
Flowers: Summer; small, white-creamy petals; fragrant
Fruit: Autumn – winter; oval, fleshy pulp
Utilization: Shade used, particularly by elephant, impala & nyala; pods used by many animals – birds, monkeys, baboons & herbivores

A	E	I	M
B	F	J	N
C	G	K	O
D	H	L	P

467
Baobab
Adansonia digitata

Up to 25 m; deciduous
Trunk: Huge, out of proportion to branches
Bark: Very smooth, skin-like
Crown: Branches gnarled & twisted like roots, as if tree has been turned upside down
Flowers: Oct – Nov; large, white
Fruit: Apr – May
Utilization: Flower pulp makes a refreshing drink; browsed by elephants; fruit eaten by baboons & monkeys
• Very easy to find

Common trees & shrubs with a rather untidy appearance

Always in shrub form

190
Small-leaved Sickle-bush
Dichrostachys cinerea, subsp. *africana*

Up to 5 m; deciduous
Crown: Multi-stemmed; sometimes dense, round and untidy; lateral twigs modified, thorn-like, in pairs
Leaves: Similar to *Acacias*
Flowers: Sep – Feb; small, bottle-brush; orange & pink
Fruit: Summer/autumn; twisted, intertwined, sickle-shaped
Utilization: Heavily browsed; pods highly nutritious

A	E	I	M
B	F	J	N
C	G	K	O
D	H	L	P

A	E	I	M
B	F	J	N
C	G	K	O
D	H	L	P

595
Magic Guarri
Euclea divinorum

6 m; evergreen
Crown: Multi-stemmed shrub/small tree; often in large stands
Leaves: Slender, grey-green; undulating edges; hard, thick
Flowers: Aug – Oct; Small dense groups in leaf axils; (M) & (F) separate
Fruit: Apr – May; Small, very hard, round, dull red-brown
Utilization: Very seldom browsed

Always in shrub form

A	E	I	M
B	F	J	N
C	G	K	O
D	H	L	P

458, 459.1, 459.2, 460, 463.1, 463.2
Raisin Bushes
Grewia species

A number of similar species occur; this illustration represents the numbers above; in right habitat occur in large numbers

Shrubs 2-5 m; deciduous
Crown: Multi-stemmed; branches thin, wavy; in some species rectangular in cross-section (not round)
Leaves: Silvery tinge, whiter underside in some species
Flowers: Summer; mainly yellow
Fruit: Smallish, some single & round, others with 4 fused fruits (cross-berries); high sugar & protein content
Utilization: Browsed by a variety of game; fruit eaten by birds & animals

A	E	I	M
B	F	J	N
C	G	K	O
D	H	L	P

621
Narrow-leaved Mustard-tree (Transvaal Mustard Tree)
Salvadora angustifolia, subsp. *australis*

Up to 7 m; evergreen
Crown: Sparse, spreading, twiggy; lower branches on the ground; stem short, crooked
Leaves: Simple; buff-green; in pairs; brittle; salty taste
Flowers: Aug; inconspicuous, greenish-yellow
Fruit: Nov – Dec; small
Utilization: Important food plant for browsers; edible fruit

Shrub or tree form

Geology, land-shape and rainfall determine the size of certain trees. In Kruger, these trees occur in large and small forms.

A	E	I	M
B	F	J	N
C	G	K	O
D	H	L	P

198
Mopane
Colophospermum mopane

From multi-stemmed shrub (2 m) to tree (18 m); deciduous
Habitat: Both tree & shrub unmistakable because they dominate particular Ecozones
Leaves: Jul – Aug leaves turn yellowish to pale-brown; look like a butterfly with open wings
Flowers: Dec – Jan; small, yellowish-green, inconspicuous
Fruit: Apr – May; flat, semi-circular in shape; pale-brown; single-seeded
Utilization: Heavily browsed, especially by elephant
• ***Very easy to find***

447
Buffalo-thorn Jujube
Ziziphus mucronata, subsp. *mucronata*

Afrikaans name: "Wag 'n bietjie" (Wait-a-bit thorn)
Up to 9 m; deciduous
Crown: Branchlets very noticeable zigzags
Leaves: Thin, curling in on upper surface; very glossy, yellow-green to dark-green
Thorns: In pairs; 1 straight, 1 curved backwards
Flowers: Oct – Feb
Fruit: Jan – Jul; berries yellow-reddish/brown
Utilization: Browsed extensively; edible fruit

A	E	I	M
B	F	J	N
C	G	K	O
D	H	L	P

237
Round-leaved Bloodwood (Round-leafed Teak)
Pterocarpus rotundifolius, subsp. *rotundifolius*

Up to 15 m; deciduous
Shrubs occur in massed clumps; single-stemmed trees rare
Leaves: Compound; large, round, glossy, dark-green
Flowers: Nov – Dec or later; yellow clusters
Pods: Ripen late summer – autumn
Utilization: Browsed especially by elephant

A	E	I	M
B	F	J	N
C	G	K	O
D	H	L	P

550
Purple-pod Cluster-leaf (Thorny Cluster-leaf)
Terminalia prunioides

Shrub to small tree; 9 m; deciduous
Crown: Sparse with loose branches; side twigs end in thorn-like protrusions
Leaves: Clustered spirally around branchlets
Flowers: Sep – Feb
Fruit: Feb – May; often more than once in a season
Utilization: Poorly browsed

A	E	I	M
B	F	J	N
C	G	K	O
D	H	L	P

"Utilization" means to what extent leaves and bark are eaten by browsers.

Unless you are in a camp or in an area marked on the Maps, you must stay in your car at all times.

The mammals, birds, reptiles and insects that visitors are most likely to see in Kruger are illustrated on the following pages.

Chacma Baboons are omnivorous feeders, see page 22

The cheetah, the world's fastest mammal, can reach a speed of 110 km/h, see page 26.

Dung Beetles carry animal dung below the surface to fertilise the soil. It is essential that nutrients originally derived from plants (when eaten by animals) are recycled back into the soil as food for the vegetation.

The cycles created by the need for food are endless. The eggs of the Guinea Fowl are food for the leguaan, while he too is a meal for the Martial Eagle. Tiny canaries eat grass seeds. This grass also feeds large waterbuck and hides Wild Dogs.

Do not upset or frighten any animal.

The conspicuous bateleur is a scavenger and raptor (meat-eater), see page 29.

Giraffe are commonly sighted in Kruger.

Scavenging hyaenas at the carcass of a hippo, killed by lions, see page 26

ANIMALS

Most animals spend a great deal of their waking hours gathering sufficient food for survival for themselves and often for their young too. When looking for animals, look near their food source.

All animals (mammals, birds, reptiles and insects) can be classified according to their method of feeding into one of the following categories.

They are either
- insectivorous (eating insects),
- herbivorous (eating vegetable matter),
- carnivorous (eating meat) or
- omnivorous (eating all forms of food).

Grazers
Grazers, like zebra, wildebeest and buffalo, are animals of the grassland. They are hunted by lion and cheetah who stalk, run and pounce. Grazing animals, in large herds and on open plains, escape from predators through their speed. There is also protection simply in the number of individuals who are alert... and available to be taken! The principle of group protection also applies to seed-eating birds.

Browsers
Browsers, like bushbuck, steenbok, duiker and nyala are found in the bushier areas of the Kruger National Park. These buck are hunted by leopards, who hide, well camouflaged, and pounce suddenly. In woody, bushy areas, both the predator's and the antelope's camouflage tend to be spots or soft stripy lines to conceal them among the leaves and branches. Here you will also find impala, who browse and graze, depending on the availability of food.

Animals on the plains
Animals on the plains have camouflage to blur the outlines between individuals. This makes the herd appear as a solid mass, which reduces the chance of a lion picking out a single individual. Try half closing your eyes as you look at a herd of zebra, and see the effect!

Water and animals
Water, like land, has an infinite, interdependent number of food cycles. Frogs are generally insectivorous, while terrapins are one of the scavengers that keep the water clean.

Olive Toad, see page 38

To help you to become familiar with as many common species as possible, and as fast as possible, the following pages are laid out in such a way that you can easily compare species that are similar.

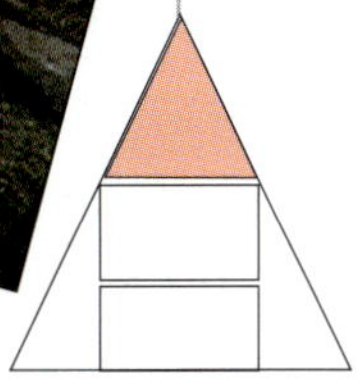

Mammals

These pages are designed to help you to look for animals in the right places and to identify them when you see them. To help you recognise the main differences between similar animals, they have been grouped together.

To help you judge the size of the mammals, they are recorded as follows:
Height: Ground to shoulder in centimetres or metres
Length: Tip of nose – tip of tail in centimetres or metres
Weight: In grams or kilograms
(M) = Male; (F) = Female

Many species of animals lay eggs, but all mammals give birth to young which are milk-fed by the mother. This leads to mother-child bonding, with the mother protecting the young. Generally, therefore, mammals give birth to fewer young than insects or reptiles and, to ensure their survival, they take care of them until they are mature enough to fend for themselves.

Small mammals

There are many species of interesting small mammals in the KNP. They live in every kind of habitat from underground to high in the branches. They eat every type of living material from plants to insects and meat.

Diurnal

You can mostly see these animals during the day

Chacma Baboon
Papio ursinus
(M) 1,4 m, (F) 1,1 m (length);
(M) 30 kg, (F) 16 kg
Habitat: Savannah; mountains
Grouping: Gregarious; up to 50 in a troop
Breeding: All year, mainly in summer; 1, rarely 2 young
Diet: Omnivorous; berries; fruit; seeds; buds; eggs of birds; insects

A	E	I	M
B	F	J	N
C	G	K	O
D	H	L	P

Vervet Monkey
Cercopithecus aethiops
1 m (length); 5 kg
Habitat: Riverine vegetation & bushy areas; near permanent water
Grouping: Gregarious; troops up to 20
Breeding: Mostly Dec – Feb; 1, rarely 2 young
Diet: Fruit; flowers; seed pods; insects; young birds; eggs

A	E	I	M
B	F	J	N
C	G	K	O
D	H	L	P

Tree Squirrel
Paraxerus cepapi
35 cm (length); 190 g
Habitat: Throughout the KNP; especially tree savannah
Grouping: Solitary or pairs
Breeding: All year; 2-3 young
Diet: Fruit seeds; shoots; roots; insects

A	E	I	M
B	F	J	N
C	G	K	O
D	H	L	P

Dwarf Mongoose
Helogale parvula
38 cm (length); 260 g
Habitat: Open savannah with termitaria or other hiding places
Grouping: Gregarious; groups of 20 or more
Breeding: Summer months; 2-4 young
Diet: Insects; beetles & their larvae; snakes; snails; birds' eggs

A	E	I	M
B	F	J	N
C	G	K	O
D	H	L	P

Banded Mongoose
Mungos mungo
55 cm (length); 1,3 kg
Habitat: Closed savannah in thickets; rocky outcrops
Grouping: Gregarious; packs up to 30 or more
Breeding: Oct – Feb; 2-6 young
Diet: Millipedes; centipedes; spiders; insects; termites; carrion; snakes; wild fruit

A	E	I	M
B	F	J	N
C	G	K	O
D	H	L	P

Nocturnal

You can mostly see these animals at dawn and dusk

Lesser Bushbaby
Galago moholi
40 cm (length); 150 g
Habitat: Savannah, especially Acacia
Grouping: Singly, or small family groups
Breeding: Summer; 2-3 young
Diet: Insects; wild berries; flowers

A	E	I	M
B	F	J	N
C	G	K	O
D	H	L	P

Thick-tailed Bushbaby
Otolemur crassicaudatus
60 cm (length); 1,1 kg
Habitat: Live in trees; well-wooded areas
Grouping: Solitary; pairs or small famiy groups
Breeding: First 3 weeks Nov; 2, occasionally 3 young
Diet: Omnivorous; berries; fruits;insects; leafy shoots; gum;small animals; birds & birds' eggs

A	E	I	M
B	F	J	N
C	G	K	O
D	H	L	P

Scrub Hare
Lepus saxatilis
55 cm (length); 2 kg
Habitat: Open savannah;
Grouping: Single; occasionally pairs
Breeding: All year; 1-3 young
Diet: Grass

A	E	I	M
B	F	J	N
C	G	K	O
D	H	L	P

Antbear (Aardvark)
Orycteropus afer
1,6 m (length); 52 kg
Habitat: Throughout the KNP
Grouping: Usually solitary
Breeding: Late winter, early spring; 1 young
Diet: Insectivorous

A	E	I	M
B	F	J	N
C	G	K	O
D	H	L	P

A	E	I	M
B	F	J	N
C	G	K	O
D	H	L	P

Porcupine
Hystrix africaeaustralis
76 cm (length); 14 kg
Habitat: Throughout the KNP; favour broken country
Grouping: Solitary or pairs
Breeding: Autumn or early winter; 1-3 young
Diet: Roots; bulbs; wild fruit

Look out for fascinating bats! You can see them during the day sleeping in large trees, under bridges, in crevices or flying around camps in the evening.

Herbivores

Browsers eat bark, leaves, buds, fruit, pods and flowers that are found in bushy areas of the KNP. Grazers eat grass as their main diet. A few animals, like impala and elephant, both graze and browse. Some herbivores depend on water every day and are found near major rivers and dams; others, like klipspringer, can survive for long periods using only the liquid from plants.

Grazers

A	E	I	M
B	F	J	N
C	G	K	O
D	H	L	P

Buffalo
Syncerus caffer
1,6 m (height); 750 kg
Habitat: Open savannah; permanent water supply
Grouping: Gregarious, herds up to 500; bulls often solitary
Breeding: Mar – May; 1 calf
Diet: Grazers; tall, coarse grass

African Elephant
Loxodonta africana
2,8 m (height); (M) 5 750 kg, (F) 3 800 kg
Habitat: Closed savannah
Grouping: Family herds led by matriarch; mature bulls solitary or in separate groups
Breeding: All year; 1 calf
Diet: Large quantities of grass when available; shoots; roots; bark; leaves; fruits

A	E	I	M
B	F	J	N
C	G	K	O
D	H	L	P

A	E	I	M
B	F	J	N
C	G	K	O
D	H	L	P

Blue Wildebeest
Connochaetes taurinus
(M) 1,5 m, (F) 1,35 m (height); (M) 250 kg, (F) 180 kg
Habitat: Open plains; short grass
Grouping: Highly gregarious; can form large herds; normally 2-15
Breeding: End Nov – Jan; 1 calf
Diet: Grazers; primarily short grass

Plains Zebra (Burchell's Zebra)
Equus quagga antiquorum
1,3 m (height); 230 kg
Habitat: Open savannah;regular water supply
Grouping: Gregarious, family groups
Breeding: Oct – Mar (with peak Dec – Feb); 1 foal
Diet: Grazers; particularly taller grass

A	E	I	M
B	F	J	N
C	G	K	O
D	H	L	P

Giraffe
Giraffa camelopardalis
3,3 m (height); 1 200 kg
Habitat: Closed savannah; daily water not essential
Breeding: All year; 1 calf (rarely 2)
Diet: Browsers, particularly Acacia leaves

A	E	I	M
B	F	J	N
C	G	K	O
D	H	L	P

Browsers

A	E	I	M
B	F	J	N
C	G	K	O
D	H	L	P

Hippopotamus
Hippopotamus amphibius
1,5 m (height); 1 500 kg
Habitat: Permanent pools; rivers with good grass cover on the banks; during day in water or resting on river-banks; graze on land at night
Grouping: Gregarious; herds about 15, with dominant bull
Breeding: All year (with summer peak); 1 calf
Diet: Grazers

A	E	I	M
B	F	J	N
C	G	K	O
D	H	L	P

Black Rhino
Diceros bicornis
1,6 m (height); 800-1100 kg
Pointed lip, head held high for browsing
Habitat: Closed savannah; prefer thickets
Grouping: Solitary; (M) territorial; (F) with offspring up to 3 years old
Breeding: All year, especially in summer; 1 calf
Diet: Browsers; twigs;leaves; forbs

Warthog
Phacochoerus aethiopicus
(M) 70 cm, (F) 60 cm (height); (M) 80 kg, (F) 55 kg
Habitat: Open savannah; with short grass
Grouping: Family groups
Breeding: Oct – Dec; 3-4 piglets
Diet: Mixed feeder; roots; tubers; fruit; short grass

A	E	I	M
B	F	J	N
C	G	K	O
D	H	L	P

White Rhino
Ceratotherium simum
1,8 m (height); (M) 2 300 kg, (F) 1 600 kg
Square lip, head hangs low for grazing
Habitat: Flat open plains; short grass; permanent water
Grouping: Territorial; small family groups
Breeding: All year; 1 calf (3-year intervals)
Diet: Grazers; fond of Guinea grass
N.B. There is no colour difference between White and Black Rhinos.

A	E	I	M
B	F	J	N
C	G	K	O
D	H	L	P

Sally MacLarty

Herbivores (continued)

A	E	I	M
B	F	J	N
C	G	K	O
D	H	L	P

Impala
Apyceros melampus
(M) 91 cm, (F) 85 cm (height); (M) 65 kg, (F) 45 kg
Habitat: Near permanent water where veld is intensely grazed
Grouping: Herds 20-400; led by dominant ram; (M) join bachelor herds at 2 yrs old
Breeding: Mid Nov – mid Jan; 1 lamb annually
Diet: Browsers & grazers; particularly grass in disturbed areas

Mountain Reedbuck
Redunca fulvorufula
70-75 cm (height); (M) 30 kg, (F) 28 kg
Habitat: Mountainous areas with good grass cover; especially in the south west of the KNP
Grouping: Herds of 3-6, up to 15; active early morning and late afternoon
Breeding: Sep – Mar; 1 calf
Diet: Grazers; often seen on burnt areas after rains

A	E	I	M
B	F	J	N
C	G	K	O
D	H	L	P

Grazers

A	E	I	M
B	F	J	N
C	G	K	O
D	H	L	P

Common Reedbuck
Redunca arundinum
(M) 90 cm, (F) 80 cm (height); (M) 80 kg, (F) 70 kg
Habitat: Near water, with stands of tall grass or reedbeds
Grouping: Pairs or family groups
Breeding: Dec – May; 1 lamb
Diet: Grazers; mainly longer grass

Browsers

A	E	I	M
B	F	J	N
C	G	K	O
D	H	L	P

Nyala
Tragelaphus angasii
(M) 1,1 m, (F) 1 m (height); (M) 110 kg, (F) 75 kg
Habitat: Riverine bush common along Luvuvhu River
Grouping: Groups of 2-5
Breeding: Sep – Mar; 1 lamb
Diet: Mainly browsers; eat more grass than kudu

Bushbuck
Tragelaphus scriptus
70-80 cm (height); (M) 60 kg, (F) 35 kg
Habitat: Riverine thickets; dense undergrowth
Grouping: Solitary, small groups
Breeding: Oct – Nov; 1 lamb
Diet: Mainly browsers

A	E	I	M
B	F	J	N
C	G	K	O
D	H	L	P

Kudu
Tragelaphus strepsiceros
(M) 1,4 m, (F) 1,25 m (height); (M) 200-260 kg, (F) 150 kg
Habitat: Closed savannah; hilly terrain
Grouping: Family groups up to 12
Breeding: Mar – Apr; 1 calf
Diet: Mainly browsers

A	E	I	M
B	F	J	N
C	G	K	O
D	H	L	P

Klipspringer
Oreotragus oreotragus
60 cm (height); (M) 11 kg, (F) 13 kg
Habitat: Rocky outcrops
Grouping: Territorial; pairs; small family groups
Breeding: All year; 1 lamb
Diet: Browsers; fruits; only drink water when available

A	E	I	M
B	F	J	N
C	G	K	O
D	H	L	P

Grazers

Waterbuck
Kobus ellipsiprymnus

(M) 1,7 m, (F) 1,3 m (height);
(M) 260 kg, (F) 230 kg
Habitat: Close to water; more open areas; tall to medium grass; hilly areas
Grouping: Herds of 10-30
Breeding: All year; peak Jan – Mar; 1 calf
Diet: Grazers

A	E	I	M
B	F	J	N
C	G	K	O
D	H	L	P

Sable Antelope
Hippotragus niger

1,35 m (height);
(M) 250 kg, (F) 210 kg
Habitat: Open savannah with tall grass; prefer granitic areas
Grouping: Few individuals; herds up to 40
Breeding: Feb – Mar; 1 calf
Diet: Mainly grazers; preferably grass taller than 8 cm

A	E	I	M
B	F	J	N
C	G	K	O
D	H	L	P

Roan Antelope
Hippotragus equinus

(M) 1,55 m, (F) 1,45 m (height);
(M) 280 kg, (F) 250 kg
Habitat: Open savannah with tall grass; especially north of Letaba River
Grouping: Herds up to 12
Breeding: All year; 1 calf
Diet: Grazers; particularly medium-tall grass

A	E	I	M
B	F	J	N
C	G	K	O
D	H	L	P

Tsessebe
Damaliscus lunatus

1,2 m (height);
(M) 140 kg, (F) 120 kg
Habitat: Open savannah especially north of Letaba River
Grouping: Small herds of 4-10
Breeding: Mid Sep – early Nov; 1 calf
Diet: Grazers; medium-height grass; avoid over-grazed areas

A	E	I	M
B	F	J	N
C	G	K	O
D	H	L	P

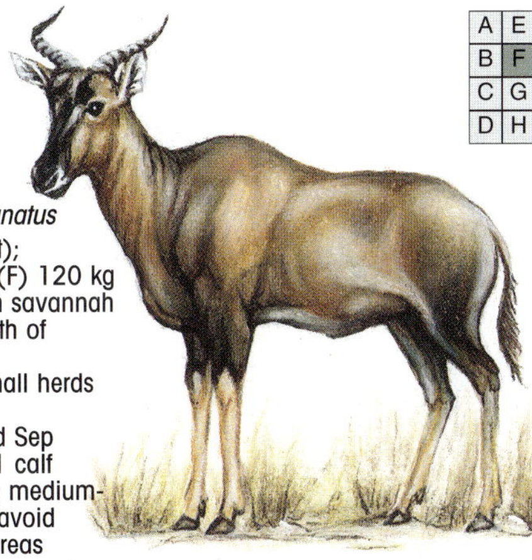

Lichtenstein's Hartebeest
Sigmoceros lichtensteinii

1,25 m (height);
170-180 kg
Habitat: Open savannah; far north; open woodlands
Grouping: Territorial males; small herds up to 10
Breeding: Peak Sep; 1 calf
Diet: Grazers

A	E	I	M
B	F	J	N
C	G	K	O
D	H	L	P

Browsers

Eland
Taurotragus oryx

(M) 1,7 m, (F) 1,5 m (height);
(M) 700 kg, (F) 450 kg
Largest Southern African antelope
Habitat: Open savannah; especially north of Olifants River
Grouping: Small family groups; sometimes join together in larger herds
Breeding: All year, peak Sep – Nov; 1 calf
Diet: Browsers

A	E	I	M
B	F	J	N
C	G	K	O
D	H	L	P

Common Duiker
Sylvicapra grimmia

(M) 50 cm, (F) 52 cm (height);
(M) 18 kg, (F) 20 kg
Habitat: Thickets along water courses
Grouping: Solitary or pairs; usually secretive
Breeding: All year; 1 lamb
Diet: Mainly browsers; also grass & fruits

A	E	I	M
B	F	J	N
C	G	K	O
D	H	L	P

Steenbok
Raphicerus campestris

50-60 cm (height);
± 11 kg
Habitat: Plains in open savannah with short to medium-height grass
Grouping: Territorial; solitary; pairs briefly for mating
Breeding: All year; 1 lamb
Diet: Mainly browsers

A	E	I	M
B	F	J	N
C	G	K	O
D	H	L	P

Sharpe's Grysbok
Raphicerus sharpei

50 cm (height); 8 kg
Habitat: Broken & hilly country; along eastern watercourses; prefer areas with low vegetation
Grouping: Solitary
Breeding: All year; 1 lamb
Diet: Mainly browsers

A	E	I	M
B	F	J	N
C	G	K	O
D	H	L	P

MICHAEL THAYER

Carnivores

These pages describe the meat-eaters that you are most likely to see and where, and how you will find them! Those which look alike have been grouped together.

Carnivores control the population numbers of herbivores. By selecting weaker animals as prey, survival of the fittest leads to healthy animals of every kind.

Further reading:
Field Guide to the Mammals of the Kruger National Park
– U de V Pienaar, S C J Joubert, A Hall-Martin, G de Graaff, I L Rautenbach
Field Guide to the Mammals of Southern Africa
– Chris & Tilde Stuart
Animals of the Kruger National Park
– G de Graaff

A	E	I	M
B	F	J	N
C	G	K	O
D	H	L	P

Diurnal

You can mostly see these animals during the day

Wild Dog
Lycaon pictus
68 cm (height); 24-30 kg
Hunt late afternoon, evening
Habitat: Adequate water; abundance of prey; areas where there are few lions or hyaenas
Grouping: Highly gregarious; packs up to 40
Breeding: May – Jul; dry winter; 2-8 pups
Diet: Small to large mammals, depending on size of pack

A	E	I	M
B	F	J	N
C	G	K	O
D	H	L	P

Cheetah
Acinonyx jubatus
75 cm (height);
(M) 50 kg, (F) 40 kg
Habitat: Open plains; savannah woodland
Grouping: Solitary, pair for mating
Breeding: All year; 2-4 cubs
Diet: Medium-small antelope; warthog; young of large mammals

Nocturnal

You can mostly see these animals at dawn and dusk

Leopard
Panthera pardus
70 cm (height);
60-80 kg
Habitat: Dense riverine bush or forest; mountains
Grouping: Solitary, except (F) with young
Breeding: All year; 2-3 cubs
Diet: Insects; fish; reptiles; baboon; impala

A	E	I	M
B	F	J	N
C	G	K	O
D	H	L	P

A	E	I	M
B	F	J	N
C	G	K	O
D	H	L	P

Side-striped Jackal
Canis adustus
38 cm (height); 8-10 kg
Habitat: Typical savannah woodlands
Grouping: Solitary in the day; but pair up before sunset
Breeding: Sep – Nov; 2-6 pups
Diet: Carrion; rodents; insects; beetles; termites; reptiles; fruits

A	E	I	M
B	F	J	N
C	G	K	O
D	H	L	P

Black-backed Jackal
Canis mesomelas
38 cm (height); 7-8 kg
Habitat: Relatively dry conditions; savannah & woodlands
Grouping: Singly, pairs or parties
Breeding: Spring & summer; 4-9 pups
Diet: Carrion; small mammals; rodents; ground-nesting birds; reptiles; insects

A	E	I	M
B	F	J	N
C	G	K	O
D	H	L	P

Clawless Otter
Aonyx capensis
1.3 m (length); 13 kg
Habitat: Quiet backwaters; thick vegetation alongside water
Grouping: Solitary or in pairs
Breeding: Mar – Apr; 2-3 pups
Diet: Crabs; molluscs; fish; aquatic birds; rodents; frogs

Hyaena
Crocuta crocuta
70-80 cm (height);
65-70 kg
Habitat: Savannah plains
Grouping: Clans of between 5 & 20
Breeding: All year; 2-3 pups
Diet: Predator & scavenger; bones

A	E	I	M
B	F	J	N
C	G	K	O
D	H	L	P

Lion
Panthera leo
1 m (height); (M) 180-230 kg, (F) 113-160 kg
Habitat: Very wide range depending on food supply
Grouping: Highly social; small family prides to big groups
Breeding: All year; 2-3 cubs
Diet: Medium-large hoofed animals; carrion
N.B. You can see lions during the day, at dusk & at dawn.

A	E	I	M
B	F	J	N
C	G	K	O
D	H	L	P

Nocturnal

You can mostly see these animals at dawn and dusk

Serval
Felis serval
50 cm (height); 10-13 kg
Habitat: Reedbeds; tall grass; low bush
Grouping: Pairs or single
Breeding: Summer; 2-4 kittens
Diet: Rodents; reptiles; insects; birds; frogs; wild fruits

A	E	I	M
B	F	J	N
C	G	K	O
D	H	L	P

A	E	I	M
B	F	J	N
C	G	K	O
D	H	L	P

Caracal
Felis caracal
40 cm (height); (M) 13 kg, (F) 10 kg
Habitat: Thick bush & rocky outcrops
Grouping: Solitary; pair briefly for mating
Breeding: In summer months; 2-4 cubs
Diet: Birds; small mammals; rodents

A	E	I	M
B	F	J	N
C	G	K	O
D	H	L	P

Spotted Genet
Genetta genetta
95 cm (length); ±2 kg
Both Large-spotted and Small-spotted genets are found in the KNP
Habitat: Widespread; especially savannah regions with high rainfall
Grouping: Mainly solitary
Breeding: Wet summer months; 2-3 kittens
Diet: Small & large mammals

Civet
Civettictis civetta
1,3 m (length); 10 kg
Habitat: Well-watered grassland
Grouping: Generally solitary
Breeding: Wet summer months; 2-3 cubs
Diet: Omnivorous; insects; wild fruit; birds; rodents; fish

A	E	I	M
B	F	J	N
C	G	K	O
D	H	L	P

Striped Polecat
Ictonyx striatus
62 cm (length); (M) 95 g, (F) 70 g
Habitat: Holes in the ground; rocky crevices; dense bush
Grouping: Singly, pairs or mothers with young
Breeding: Oct – Nov; 1-3 kittens
Diet: Rodents; reptiles; insects; birds; frogs; snakes

A	E	I	M
B	F	J	N
C	G	K	O
D	H	L	P

A	E	I	M
B	F	J	N
C	G	K	O
D	H	L	P

African Wild Cat
Felis lybica
38 cm (height); 4-5 kg
Habitat: Wide spread; tall grass & thick bush
Grouping: Solitary, but may hunt in pairs
Breeding: Summer months; litter up to 5 kittens
Diet: Rodents; birds; reptiles; insects; hares; fruit

A	E	I	M
B	F	J	N
C	G	K	O
D	H	L	P

Honey Badger
Mellivora capensis
95 cm (length); 12 kg
Habitat: Very wide spread
Grouping: Generally solitary
Breeding: Spring – summer; 2 pups
Diet: Reptiles; insects; larvae of dung beetles; eggs; ground birds; wild fruits; honey

Sally MacLarty

Birds

Nearly 500 species of birds have been identified in the Kruger National Park.

You will add interest to your hour, and your day, by spotting a bird that you have never seen before!

This list contains 90 of the more common birds that you are likely to see and identify, most of the year round.

Birds are more easily identified if you know where to find them. Specific species live in a particular area or habitat. To help you look, the following pages show groupings of birds in their most likely habitats, e.g. African Fish Eagles and Green Pigeons are usually found in trees near permanent water, such as rivers or large dams.

To see birds, large mammals and reptiles in their natural environment you need to visit a wildlife reserve. Smaller birds are the one species that you can carry on watching after leaving the KNP. Start by learning a few of the more colourful and easy-to-spot species and you will find pleasure for years to come, wherever you are.

All birds listed below are:

- ❑ resident & breed locally
- ❑ solitary or in pairs (unless otherwise stated)
- ❑ numbered with a "Roberts" number

Bird sizes are measured:

- ❑ from the beak-tip to the tail-tip, or toe-tip (whichever is longer)

(M) = Male; (F) = Female

Further reading:
Field Guide to the Birds of the Kruger National Park
– Ian Sinclair & Ian Whyte
Roberts' Birds of Southern Africa
– Gordon Lindsay MacLean
Birds of the Kruger National Park
– Kenneth Newman

Birds in dry bushveld

Hunting from a perch

447
Lilac-breasted Roller
Coracias caudata

A	E	I	M
B	F	J	N
C	G	K	O
D	H	L	P

36 cm
Breeding: Characteristic rolling flight in the breeding season (from which name stems)
Diet: Insects; small snakes; lizards; rodents

735
Magpie Shrike (Long-tailed Shrike)
Cornivella melanoleuca
45 cm
Long tails are jerked while birds call from prominent perch
Grouping: Sociable small groups; 3-10 birds
Diet: Insects; small reptiles

A	E	I	M
B	F	J	N
C	G	K	O
D	H	L	P

435
Brown-hooded Kingfisher
Halcyon albiventris
23 cm
Bush kingfisher; perch conspicuously to search for prey; not known to eat fish in the KNP
Breeding: Excavate nests out of sandbanks; make a chamber at the end of a 1 m tunnel
Diet: Mostly insects; also invertebrates

A	E	I	M
B	F	J	N
C	G	K	O
D	H	L	P

A	E	I	M
B	F	J	N
C	G	K	O
D	H	L	P

541
Fork-tailed Drongo
Dicrurus adsimilis
24 cm
Very common; aggressive; mob larger raptors that enter territory; follow antelope to catch flushed insects; often seen perched prominently in trees
Diet: Mainly insects

433
Woodland Kingfisher
Halcyon senegalensis
23 cm
Summer migrant; has very characteristic call *"krit-trrrrrr"*, heard in summer months
Habitat: Lives in woodland (as name suggests), not necessarily near water
Diet: Mainly insects; also lizards, snakes, frogs

A	E	I	M
B	F	J	N
C	G	K	O
D	H	L	P

With antelope

772
Red-billed Oxpecker
Buphagus erythrorhynchus
21 cm
Most common oxpecker in the KNP; warn host animals by flying away noisily when sensing danger
Grouping: Small groups 2-6
Diet: Mostly ticks; also horseflies, other insects

A	E	I	M
B	F	J	N
C	G	K	O
D	H	L	P

A	E	I	M
B	F	J	N
C	G	K	O
D	H	L	P

756
White-crowned Shrike
Eurocephalus anguitimens
24 cm
Habitat: Perch conspicuously
Grouping: Small scattered groups; up to 12 birds
Diet: Insects

A	E	I	M
B	F	J	N
C	G	K	O
D	H	L	P

444
Little Bee-eater
Merops bullockoides
17 cm
Stalk flying insects by fast flight from perch; use same perch day after day
Grouping: Solitary or pairs by day; small groups roosting in branches at night
Diet: Flying insects

You will get more enjoyment from bird watching if you use a pair of binoculars.

On a prominent perch

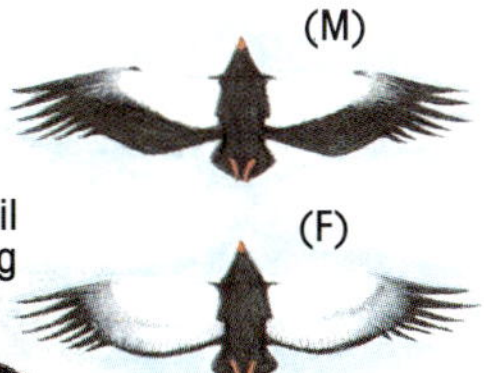

146
Bateleur *Terathopius ecaudatus*

55-70 cm
Very conspicuous raptor due to short tail & colour of face & feet; often seen flying with side-to-side, tight-rope walker flight action
Diet: Carrion; birds; mammals up to 4 kg

A	E	I	M
B	F	J	N
C	G	K	O
D	H	L	P

126
Yellow-billed Kite
Milvus aegyptius

55 cm
Summer breeding migrant; scavenge actively, especially on roads, at camps & picnic sites; very common where termites emerge
Diet: Carrion; insects; crustaceans; small mammals; reptiles

A	E	I	M
B	F	J	N
C	G	K	O
D	H	L	P

A	E	I	M
B	F	J	N
C	G	K	O
D	H	L	P

89
Marabou Stork
Leptoptilos crumeniferus

1,5 m
These birds are scavengers; only occur where enough carrion is available, therefore seldom seen outside KNP
Grouping: Usually gregarious
Diet: Mostly carrion; also birds & fish when large numbers are readily available

A	E	I	M
B	F	J	N
C	G	K	O
D	H	L	P

140
Martial Eagle
Polemaetus bellicosus

80 cm
Largest eagle in Africa; hunt on the wing, or from a perch; very large powerful talons to grasp prey
Diet: Larger birds; small mammals (duiker size); reptiles, especially monitors

A	E	I	M
B	F	J	N
C	G	K	O
D	H	L	P

124
Lappet-faced Vulture
Torgos tracheliotus

1 m
Biggest vulture; dominant over other vultures at carcass, but do not necessarily compete with them
Diet: Carrion, including tough skin & ligaments; also kill small mammals; barbel

A	E	I	M
B	F	J	N
C	G	K	O
D	H	L	P

527
Lesser-striped Swallow
Hirundo abyssinica

16 cm
More common in summer; striped breasts make them easy to identify
Habitat: Near bridges, road culverts & buildings
Grouping: Pairs; small flocks
Diet: Flying insects

In the sky

A	E	I	M
B	F	J	N
C	G	K	O
D	H	L	P

417
Little Swift
Apus affinis

14 cm
Vocal, particularly in the evenings; feed, drink & gather nesting material while flying
Grouping: Highly gregarious; big flocks mix with other swifts & swallows
Diet: Insects & spiders

142
Brown Snake Eagle
Circaetus cinereus

A	E	I	M
B	F	J	N
C	G	K	O
D	H	L	P

75 cm
Legs not feathered, as need heavy scales for protection against snake bites
Grouping: Usually solitary
Diet: Snakes up to 3 m long; monitors; smaller lizards

123
White-backed Vulture
Gyps africanus

94 cm
Most common vulture; like most vultures have excellent eyesight to find food; occur in large numbers at kills
Grouping: Gregarious, breed in trees in loose colonies
Diet: Carrion (often chase smaller vultures off carrion)

A	E	I	M
B	F	J	N
C	G	K	O
D	H	L	P

Birds in dry bushveld (continued)

In large trees

A	E	I	M
B	F	J	N
C	G	K	O
D	H	L	P

373
Grey Lourie
Corythaixoides concolor
49 cm
Called *"go away bird"* because of call
Grouping: Pairs; small parties
Diet: Fruit; flower-buds; insects; leaves; seeds

A	E	I	M
B	F	J	N
C	G	K	O
D	H	L	P

464
Black-collared Barbet
Lybius torquatus
20 cm
(M) & (F) call in ringing duet perched prominently on tree
Grouping: Solitary or pairs; small groups
Breeding: Nest is a hole, often in underside of dead branch
Diet: Fruit; insects

740
Puffback
Dryoscopus cubla
18 cm

A	E	I	M
B	F	J	N
C	G	K	O
D	H	L	P

In display (M) puffs up back feathers giving it a rounder shape; hence the Afrikaans name "sneeubal" (snowball); more visible than other bush shrikes
Diet: Insects

568
Dark-capped Bulbul (Black-eyed Bulbul)
Pycnonotus barbatus
22 cm
Very common; highly vocal & restless
Grouping: Pairs; loose groups
Diet: Fruit; nectar; insects; small lizards

A	E	I	M
B	F	J	N
C	G	K	O
D	H	L	P

A	E	I	M
B	F	J	N
C	G	K	O
D	H	L	P

398
Pearl-spotted Owl
Glaucidium perlatum
19 cm
Often hunt by day; hunt by dropping onto prey; can catch bats in flight
Breeding: Breed in old barbet holes
Diet: Mostly insects; small mammals; birds; amphibians

A	E	I	M
B	F	J	N
C	G	K	O
D	H	L	P

545
Black-headed Oriole
Oriolus larvatus
25 cm
Call very distinctive; liquid piping notes often heard early in the morning
Grouping: Solitary or pairs; loose groups at food source
Diet: Insects; fruit; nectar

426
Red-faced Mousebird
Urocolius indicus
34 cm
Resemble mice as they clamber through the trees
Grouping: Gregarious; in small groups, up to 8 birds
Diet: Mainly fruit; flowers; nectar

A	E	I	M
B	F	J	N
C	G	K	O
D	H	L	P

A	E	I	M
B	F	J	N
C	G	K	O
D	H	L	P

710
Paradise Flycatcher
Terpsiphone viridis
(M) 23 cm with 18 cm tail; (F) 17 cm
Normally summer breeding migrants; hunt from perch; very active; *"chit-cheer"* call often heard
Diet: Small insects

354
Cape Turtle Dove
Streptopelia capicola
28 cm

A	E	I	M
B	F	J	N
C	G	K	O
D	H	L	P

Very common; smallest and palest of ring neck doves; call likened to *"work **harder** – work **harder**"*
Grouping: Groups & mixed parties; large numbers at food source
Diet: Seeds; insects; winged termites

353
African Mourning Dove
Streptopelia decipiens
30 cm

A	E	I	M
B	F	J	N
C	G	K	O
D	H	L	P

Call is a soft resonant *"ku-kur-rrr"*; red skin around eye distinguishes it from other doves
Habitat: Common at Letaba Camp; can be very tame
Grouping: In pairs but flocks gather at food sources
Diet: Seed & grain

Against tree trunks

A	E	I	M
B	F	J	N
C	G	K	O
D	H	L	P

452
Green Wood-Hoopoe (Red-billed Woodhoopoe)
Phoeniculus purpureus
34 cm
Loud cackling call likened to a group of women laughing; fly from tree to tree in noisy group; use long bills to probe for insects beneath bark or in holes in wood
Habitat: Prefer open *Acacia* to dense woodland
Grouping: Gregarious groups of 2-16
Diet: Insects; millipedes; lizards; nectar

A	E	I	M
B	F	J	N
C	G	K	O
D	H	L	P

486
Cardinal Woodpecker
Dendropicos fuscescens
15 cm
Small woodpecker; only (M) has red on head; tap quietly but rapidly, often in small trees; insert barbed tongue to withdraw insects
Diet: Beetle larvae & other insects

A	E	I	M
B	F	J	N
C	G	K	O
D	H	L	P

483
Golden-tailed Woodpecker
Campethera ambingoni
22 cm
(F) has less red on head; loud, echoing tap is a form of communication
Diet: Ants & larvae; other insects

On the ground

1 Ostrich
Struthio camelus

(M)

2 m
World's largest bird; prefer short grass plains, therefore mostly found in eastern half of Kruger, north of Letaba River
Grouping: Family groups
Diet: Mainly vegetarian; grass; berries; seeds

A	E	I	M
B	F	J	N
C	G	K	O
D	H	L	P

230 Kori Bustard
Ardeotis kori

(M) 1,2-1,5 m, (F) 1,0-1,2 m
World's heaviest flying bird; reluctant flyer, run before take off; occur in open plains, more often seen in eastern side of Kruger
Diet: Locusts; grasshoppers; *Acacia* gum; seeds; lizards; small rodents

A	E	I	M
B	F	J	N
C	G	K	O
D	H	L	P

463 Ground Hornbill
Bucorvus leadbeateri

1,1 m
Common throughout Kruger; have a loud resounding booming call, often heard early in the morning; on the endangered species list; mainly terrestrial, but sleep in trees
Grouping: Family groups 4-10
Diet: Entirely carnivorous; reptiles; tortoises; small mammals; snails; insects

A	E	I	M
B	F	J	N
C	G	K	O
D	H	L	P

237 Red-crested Korhaan
Eupodotis ruficrista

(M)

50 cm
Well-camouflaged in long grass; red crest is not conspicuous, except in display
Breeding: In breeding season (M) flies vertically up 10-30 m, then folds wings & falls back to ground; polygamous
Diet: Arthropods; seeds; fruit; gum

A	E	I	M
B	F	J	N
C	G	K	O
D	H	L	P

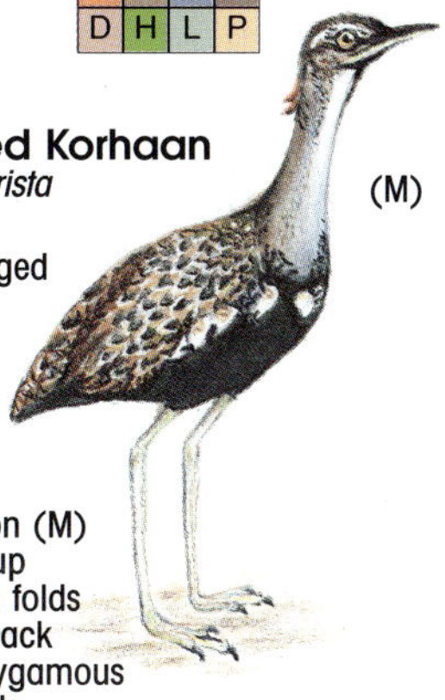

203 Helmeted Guineafowl
Numida meleagris

57 cm
Reddish-brown 'helmet' on top of head is a projection of bone; often walk in single file to water
Grouping: Highly gregarious when not breeding; flocks of hundreds of birds
Diet: Ants; termites; arthropods; tubers

A	E	I	M
B	F	J	N
C	G	K	O
D	H	L	P

196 Natal Francolin
Pternistes natalensis

36 cm
Identified by black eye, red bill & legs
Habitat: Rocky areas near water
Grouping: Pairs; groups up to 10 birds
Diet: Molluscs; insects; roots; bulbs; fruit; seeds

A	E	I	M
B	F	J	N
C	G	K	O
D	H	L	P

189 Crested Francolin
Francolinus sephaena

32 cm
Identified by black eye & bill, red legs; tail is often cocked like that of a bantam chicken; very noisy at dawn & dusk
Grouping: Pairs; small groups
Diet: Bulbs; seeds; berries; insects; molluscs

A	E	I	M
B	F	J	N
C	G	K	O
D	H	L	P

255 Crowned Lapwing (Crowned Plover)
Vanellus coronatus

30 cm
Occur throughout Kruger on heavily grazed areas; call well-known *"keefeeet"* when flying up; only plover to breed in loose colonies, probably for protection
Grouping: Gregarious; outside of breeding season up to 40 in group
Diet: Variety of insects & their larvae

A	E	I	M
B	F	J	N
C	G	K	O
D	H	L	P

199 Swainson's Spurfowl (Swainson's Francolin)
Pternistes swainsonii

(M) 38 cm, (F) 33 cm
Identified by red face & throat, brown legs
Habitat: Grassland & areas not far from water
Grouping: Solitary or pairs; small groups
Diet: Seeds; berries; shoots; roots; bulbs; insects; molluscs

A	E	I	M
B	F	J	N
C	G	K	O
D	H	L	P

347 Double-banded Sandgrouse
Pterocles bicinctus

25 cm
Along roadsides in daytime; flocks of up to 100 drink at waterholes in the evening; need a daily ration of water
Grouping: Pairs or family groups
Diet: Seeds & bulbs

A	E	I	M
B	F	J	N
C	G	K	O
D	H	L	P

A	E	I	M
B	F	J	N
C	G	K	O
D	H	L	P

Near rocky outcrops

886 Rock Bunting
Emberiza tahapisi

14 cm
Easily seen when perched prominently on rocky protrusion; nomadic when not breeding
Diet: Seeds; insects on the ground

593 Mocking Chat
Thamnolaea cinnamomeiventris

22 cm
(F) is not as colourful as (M); mimic a wide range of bird calls
Grouping: Pairs or small groups; 4-5 birds
Diet: Insects; fruit

(M)

A	E	I	M
B	F	J	N
C	G	K	O
D	H	L	P

Birds in dry bushveld (continued)

In open bush or on ground nearby

A	E	I	M
B	F	J	N
C	G	K	O
D	H	L	P

764
Cape Glossy Starling
Lamprotornis nitens
23 cm
Usually feed off the ground; also forage in trees
Grouping: Pairs breeding; non-breeding flocks 6-10
Diet: Omnivorous, mainly insects and fruit

A	E	I	M
B	F	J	N
C	G	K	O
D	H	L	P

762
Burchell's Starling
Lamprotornis australis
32 cm
Large starling; black eye; very noisy
Grouping: Solitary or pairs; small groups
Diet: Mainly insects; also fruit

A	E	I	M
B	F	J	N
C	G	K	O
D	H	L	P

765
Greater Blue-eared Starling
Lamprotornis chalybaeus
22 cm
Most common starling in Kruger
Habitat: Particularly common in camps & picnic sites; roost communally
Grouping: Breeding pairs; non-breeding gregarious in large flocks
Diet: Omnivorous, mainly fruit

A	E	I	M
B	F	J	N
C	G	K	O
D	H	L	P

459
Southern Yellow-billed Hornbill
Tockus leucomelas
48-60 cm
Habitat: Often seen in camp sites & picnic spots; forage on ground & in trees; can be tame
Grouping: Solitary or pairs; small groups
Breeding: In breeding season (Oct – Nov), pairs bob up & down while calling together
Diet: Rodents; insects; scorpions; seeds; fruit

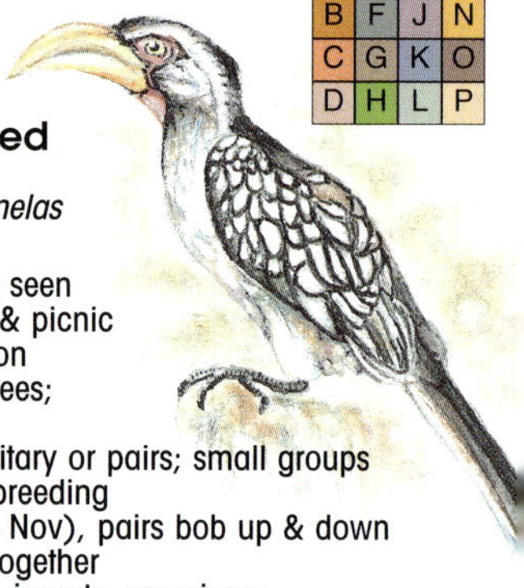

A	E	I	M
B	F	J	N
C	G	K	O
D	H	L	P

458
Red-billed Hornbill
Tockus erythrorhynchus 46 cm
Forage on ground; dig for food in soil & dung
Habitat: Overgrazed areas; Mopane woodland
Grouping: Pairs; non-breeding, gregarious, small flocks
Breeding: Like all hornbills (F) is sealed off in nest, where she loses all her feathers, during laying and incubation; during this time, she is fed by (M) through small opening
Diet: Insects; seeds; scorpions; amphibians

A	E	I	M
B	F	J	N
C	G	K	O
D	H	L	P

580
Groundscraper Thrush
Psophocichla litsipsirupa
21 cm
Most often seen on lawns of restcamps; search under leaves and debris for food – hence the name
Grouping: Solitary or pairs; sometimes groups
Diet: Insects & variety of worms; berries

A	E	I	M
B	F	J	N
C	G	K	O
D	H	L	P

842
Red-billed Firefinch
Lagonosticta senegala
10 cm
(F) more brown than (M); often seen with other seed-eaters
Habitat: Acacia thornveld with open patches near watercourses
Grouping: Pairs or small parties
Diet: Seeds

(M)

451
African Hoopoe
Upupa africana
27 cm
Conspicuous crest can be erected into fan; call from perch in tree
Grouping: Solitary or pairs; non-breeding small groups
Diet: Insects; earthworms; small snakes; frogs

A	E	I	M
B	F	J	N
C	G	K	O
D	H	L	P

846
Common Waxbill
Estrildo astrild
13 cm
Habitat: Taller, thicker grass; along rivers & dams
Grouping:
Breeding pairs or family groups; non-breeding gregarious flocks, up to 30 birds
Diet: Grass seeds, often taken green from seed-heads

A	E	I	M
B	F	J	N
C	G	K	O
D	H	L	P

A	E	I	M
B	F	J	N
C	G	K	O
D	H	L	P

844
Blue Waxbill
Uraeginthus angolensis
13 cm
Most common waxbill
Grouping: Breeding pairs; non-breeding gregarious, up to 40 birds
Breeding: Often build nest close to wasp nest for protection
Diet: Seeds on ground

On flowering plants

793
Collared Sunbird
Hedydipna collaris
11 cm
Shorter bill than most sunbirds; feed in low bush
Grouping: Usually pairs; family groups; aggressive, territorial (M)
Diet: Mainly insects

A	E	I	M
B	F	J	N
C	G	K	O
D	H	L	P

A	E	I	M
B	F	J	N
C	G	K	O
D	H	L	P

884
Golden-breasted Bunting
Emberiza flaviventris
16 cm
Very common; show white outer-tail feathers when flushed; call from perch sounds like *"pretty boy-pretty boy-pretty boy"*
Grouping: Solitary or pairs; gregarious flocks, up to 20 birds
Diet: Mainly seeds; also insects

A	E	I	M
B	F	J	N
C	G	K	O
D	H	L	P

869
Yellow-fronted Canary (Yellow-eyed Canary)
Serinus mozambicus
12 cm
Often in groups withother birds; often feeding on the ground; call likened to *"yes I see you"*
Grouping: Gregarious flocks 20-30
Diet: Seeds; insects on the ground

791
Scarlet-chested Sunbird
Nectarinia senegalensis 14 cm
(F) very drab compared with (M); more common in rest camps, where flowers grow, than in the veld
Grouping: Solitary or pairs, except at food source
Breeding: Nest consists of plant material woven together with spider webs
Diet: Mainly nectar

(M)

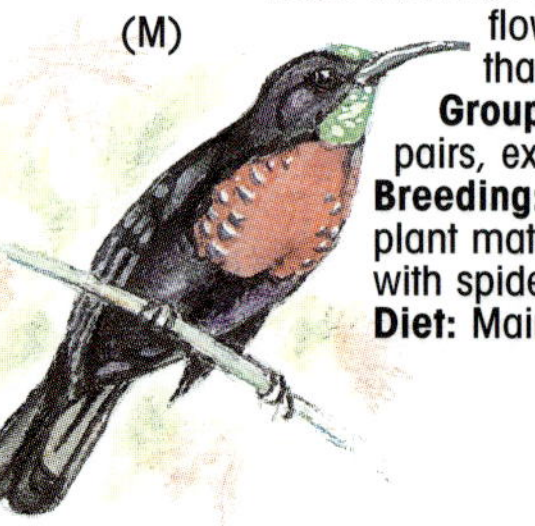

A	E	I	M
B	F	J	N
C	G	K	O
D	H	L	P

In thick bush or on ground nearby

A	E	I	M
B	F	J	N
C	G	K	O
D	H	L	P

743
Three-streaked Tchagra
Tchagra australis
19 cm
Forage low down in thickets & on the ground
Habitat: Woodland; thornveld thickets
Diet: Insects

A	E	I	M
B	F	J	N
C	G	K	O
D	H	L	P

753
White-crested Helmet-Shrike
Prionops plumatus
20 cm
Very restless birds, tend to move continuously; each group has a territory which is defended against other groups, & it has only one breeding pair
Grouping: Gregarious; groups 5-22
Diet: Insects; spiders; rarely lizards

A	E	I	M
B	F	J	N
C	G	K	O
D	H	L	P

701
Chinspot Batis
Batis molitor
13 cm
Name derived from rusty chinspot in (F); call likened to *"three blind mice"* tune
Grouping: Solitary or pairs; often in bird parties in summer
Breeding: (M) feeds (F) during courtship, nest-building, egg laying & incubation (Aug – Feb)
Diet: Insects; spiders

A	E	I	M
B	F	J	N
C	G	K	O
D	H	L	P

560
Arrow-marked Babbler
Turdoides jardineii
24 cm
Raucous chorus of birds often heard, but they are difficult to see
Habitat: Forage on ground; clamber through lower branches
Grouping: Gregarious; groups of up to 10
Diet: Mainly insects & small lizards

A	E	I	M
B	F	J	N
C	G	K	O
D	H	L	P

613
White-browed Scrub-Robin
Cercotrichas leucophrys
15 cm
Territorial; secretive, hide deep in thick bush & long grass; often sing for long periods
Grouping: Solitary
Diet: Insects; spiders; some berries; nectar

A	E	I	M
B	F	J	N
C	G	K	O
D	H	L	P

473
Crested Barbet
Trachyphonus vaillantii
23 cm
Quite inconspicuous, unless foraging on ground or calling; characteristic trill can be heard all year, especially in summer
Grouping: Solitary or pairs; small groups
Diet: Mainly insects; less fruit than other barbets

A	E	I	M
B	F	J	N
C	G	K	O
D	H	L	P

355
Laughing Dove
Streptopelia senegalensis
25 cm
Does not have black ring around neck; very common in Kruger; must drink water daily – often seen in big groups at water points
Grouping: Solitary or pairs; groups at water
Diet: Small seeds of herbs & grass; termites; small insects

A	E	I	M
B	F	J	N
C	G	K	O
D	H	L	P

358
Emerald-spotted Wood-Dove
Turtur chalcospilos
20 cm
Often found feeding next to the road; call is a distinctive bushveld sound, ending in a mournful, descending *"tu-tu-tu-tu-tu-tu-tu"*
Diet: Seeds; berries; termites

Birds active at night

Nocturnal

You can see these birds at dawn and dusk, or in the camps at night

A	E	I	M
B	F	J	N
C	G	K	O
D	H	L	P

405
Fiery-necked Nightjar
Caprimulgus pectoralis
24 cm
Call *"Good Lord, deliver us"*, especially at dusk and dawn; hawk from a perch; very wide gaping mouths
Diet: Insects, especially beetles; spiders

401
Spotted Eagle Owl
Bubo africanus
45 cm
Superb hearing; tufts on head are not ears; like other owls they can move heads 180° to see directly behind them
Habitat: Roost by day on rocky ledge or in tree; pairs often sit close together; presence is often given away by chattering of small birds
Diet: Large insects, like grasshoppers; small mammals; birds

A	E	I	M
B	F	J	N
C	G	K	O
D	H	L	P

A	E	I	M
B	F	J	N
C	G	K	O
D	H	L	P

298
Water Thick-knee
Water Dikkop
Burhinus vermiculatus
40 cm
Habitat: Seldom far from water
Grouping: Solitary; pairs or non-breeding flocks, 20-30 birds
Breeding: No nest, but lay eggs on ground among driftwood
Diet: Insects; crustaceans; molluscs

Birds near permanent water

In large trees

A	E	I	M
B	F	J	N
C	G	K	O
D	**H**	L	P

148
African Fish Eagle
Haliaeetus vocifer

70 cm
Loud distinctive call
Habitat: Spend most of the day perched in large riverine trees
Grouping: Pairs; mate for life
Diet: Fish; sometimes birds

A	E	I	M
B	F	J	N
C	G	K	O
D	**H**	L	P

815
Lesser Masked Weaver
Ploceus intermedius

15 cm
Grouping: Aug – Feb; gregarious; non-breeding (M) resembles (F)
Breeding: Large breeding colonies, often in association with Spotted-backed weavers; nests small & neat in trees overhanging water
Diet: Insects; seeds; nectar

361
Green Pigeon
Treron calva

30 cm
Resemble parrots when clambering through trees
Habitat: Secretive, feed high in evergreen trees
Grouping: Gregarious
Diet: Fruit, especially figs

A	E	I	M
B	F	J	N
C	G	K	O
D	**H**	L	P

A	E	I	M
B	F	J	N
C	G	K	O
D	**H**	L	P

371
Purple-crested Turaco (Purple-crested Lourie)
Musophaga porphyreolopha

42 cm
Very conspicuous red on wings when flying; call is loud "***kok - kok***" repeated many times
Grouping: Pairs; small groups
Breeding: Aug – Nov
Diet: Mainly fruit

In reeds

A	E	I	M
B	F	J	N
C	G	K	O
D	**H**	L	P

431
Malachite Kingfisher
Alcedo cristata

14 cm
Dive for prey from reeds & branches, overhanging quiet pools
Grouping: Solitary
Breeding: Build nests in sandy cliffs by excavating long tunnels with chambers
Diet: Fish; insects; tadpoles; frogs; crustaceans

On a prominent perch

429
Giant Kingfisher
Megaceryle maxima

46 cm
Largest of the kingfishers; distinctive brown chest; hunt from perch above water
Grouping: Solitary; rarely pairs
Diet: Fish; crabs; frogs

A	E	I	M
B	F	J	N
C	G	K	O
D	**H**	L	P

A	E	I	M
B	F	J	N
C	G	K	O
D	**H**	L	P

428
Pied Kingfisher
Ceryle rudis

28 cm
Hover above water searching for fish; stun prey before eating
Grouping: Solitary or pairs; loose groups
Diet: Mainly fish

A	E	I	M
B	F	J	N
C	G	K	O
D	**H**	L	P

443
White-fronted Bee-eater
Merops bullockoides

24 cm
Distinctive white & red throat; catch insects in the air; large groups seen in sandy river banks where they breed
Grouping: Solitary or small groups
Diet: Flying insects, especially butterflies

Near the water's edge

711
African Pied Wagtail
Motacilla aguimp

A	E	I	M
B	F	J	N
C	G	K	O
D	**H**	L	P

20 cm
Characteristic wagging of tail while searching for food
Habitat: Common on waterways & riverside camps
Grouping: Breeding pairs or groups
Diet: Small invertebrates; insects

A	E	I	M
B	F	J	N
C	G	K	O
D	**H**	L	P

94
Hadeda Ibis
Bostrychia hagedash

76 cm
The only vocal ibis; loud, clamorous "***ha-ha-de-da***"
Grouping: Gregarious; large non-breeding flocks, 5-20 birds
Diet: Mainly insects; they can also retrieve food from deep under the soil with their long bills

258
Blacksmith Plover
Vanellus armatus

A	E	I	M
B	F	J	N
C	G	K	O
D	**H**	L	P

30 cm
Name refers to call that resembles metallic ring of hammer hitting an anvil
Grouping: Pairs; non-breeding, loose flocks, up to 30
Breeding: Like other plovers, chicks leave the nest almost immediately after hatching
Diet: Insects; worms; molluscs

249
Three-banded Plover
Charadrius tricollaris

18 cm
Hunt by running short distances, then stopping to peck at prey
Grouping: Pairs; non-breeding flocks, up to 40
Breeding: Protect eggs & chicks by pretending to be injured & luring away predators
Diet: Mainly insects & spiders

A	E	I	M
B	F	J	N
C	G	K	O
D	**H**	L	P

In shallows

A	E	I	M
B	F	J	N
C	G	K	O
D	H	L	P

64 Goliath Heron
Ardea goliath

1,4 m
Largest heron in the world; hunt by standing stock-still in water waiting for prey; often seen standing knee-deep in water; call is a hoarse ***"kraak"***
Grouping: Solitary
Diet: Mostly fish of 500-600 g

A	E	I	M
B	F	J	N
C	G	K	O
D	H	L	P

62 Grey Heron
Ardea cinerea

1 m
Commonly seen wading through shallow water, stalking prey
Grouping: Solitary
Diet: Mostly fish of 10-20 g

A	E	I	M
B	F	J	N
C	G	K	O
D	H	L	P

88 Saddle-billed Stork
Ephippiorhynchus senegalensis

1,4 m
One of the endangered birds (less than 20 pairs in the KNP); every bird has a unique bill colour/pattern; notice the difference in eye colour & wattles (skin flaps) between (M) & (F)
Diet: Mainly fish

66 Great Egret (Great White Egret)
Egretta alba

95 cm
(Breeding plumage illustrated)
Stand motionless for hours in shallow water watching for prey
Grouping: Solitary
Breeding: Bills change from yellow to black just before breeding season
Diet: Fish; frogs; insects; small mammals

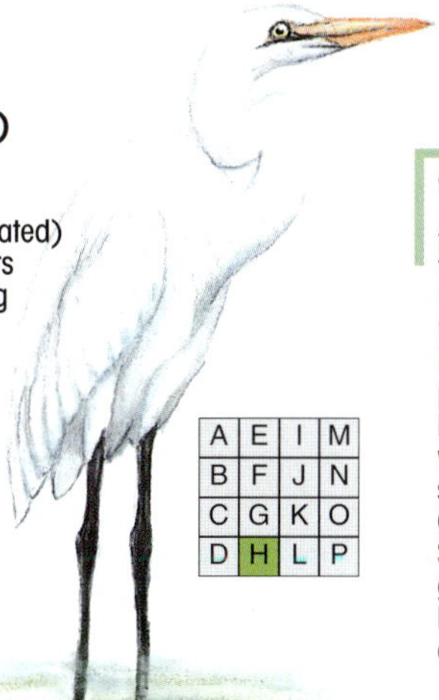

A	E	I	M
B	F	J	N
C	G	K	O
D	H	L	P

A	E	I	M
B	F	J	N
C	G	K	O
D	H	L	P

95 African Spoonbill
Platalea alba

90 cm
Feed by moving partially-opened bill from side to side through water, to sieve out small food items
Grouping: Solitary or gregarious
Diet: Small fish; aquatic invertebrates

99 White-faced Duck
Dendrocygna viduata

48 cm
Very erect posture shows white face clearly; more often seen once rains have filled seasonal pans
Grouping: Gregarious flocks of up to ± 30
Diet: Underwater seeds & tubers of aquatic plants

A	E	I	M
B	F	J	N
C	G	K	O
D	H	L	P

On water

A	E	I	M
B	F	J	N
C	G	K	O
D	H	L	P

60 African Darter
Anhinga rufa

79 cm
Swim with only head emerged, with long neck folded under water ready to spear prey; often seen sitting on perch drying wings
Grouping: Usually solitary
Diet: Fish; frogs; arthropods

A	E	I	M
B	F	J	N
C	G	K	O
D	H	L	P

55 White-breasted Cormorant
Phalacrocorax lucidus

90 cm
Not very common in Kruger, but unique as is the only cormorant with both riverine & marine populations
Grouping: Solitary or gregarious
Diet: Mainly fish

A	E	I	M
B	F	J	N
C	G	K	O
D	H	L	P

115 Comb Duck (Knob-billed Duck)
Sarkidiornis melanotos

(M) 80 cm,
(F) 65 cm
Only (M) has a knob; often seen at temporary pools after rain
Grouping: Breeding pairs or small groups
Breeding: Polygamous, 1 (M): 3 (F)
Diet: Seeds & tubers of water plants

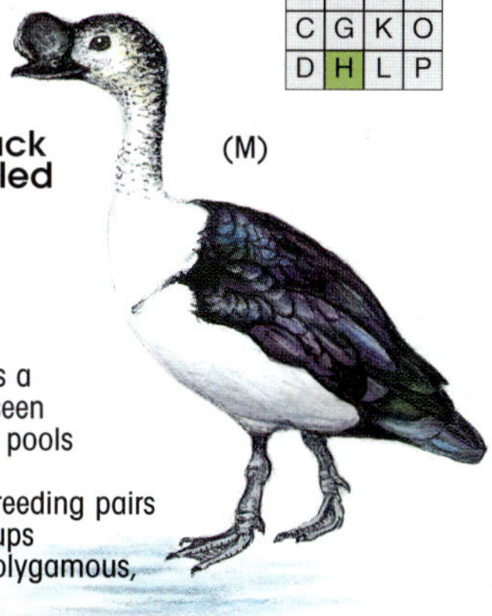

81 Hamerkop
Scopus umbretta

56 cm
Feed in shallow water (or even flood water); tread & stir mud to flush prey
Grouping: Solitary or pairs; small groups
Breeding: Huge, untidy nest, made by 1-4 birds & used for generations; superstition suggests it is unlucky to disturb a nest
Diet: Mostly tadpoles & frogs; also fish

A	E	I	M
B	F	J	N
C	G	K	O
D	H	L	P

102 Egyptian Goose
Alopochen aegyptiacus

70 cm
Very common; call often heard: (F) honks ***"honk honk haaaa"***, (M) hisses
Grouping: Pairs; non-breeding gregarious
Breeding: Use disused raptor or Hamerkop nests; also nest on rocky ledges
Diet: Grass; sedges; herbs

A	E	I	M
B	F	J	N
C	G	K	O
D	H	L	P

A	E	I	M
B	F	J	N
C	G	K	O
D	H	L	P

240 African Jacana
Actophilornis africanus

28 cm
Walk on lily pads on extraordinary long feet
Grouping: Solitary or pairs; small loose groups
Breeding: (F) has many mates in one season; (M) takes care of chicks, sometimes carrying them under wings
Diet: Mainly aquatic insects

MICHAEL THAYER

Reptiles, insects and other small creatures

The Kruger National Park is home to dozens of reptiles and thousands of species of insects. The descriptions and pictures below will help you to find some of the more obvious ones. Take note of where they occur and at what time of day to look for them. If you keep your eyes open, you will find many fascinating creatures.

To help you judge the size of the creatures, they are recorded as follows:
Length: In millimetres, centimetres or metres
Weight: In kilograms
(M) = Male; (F) = Female

Further reading:
Field Guide to Insects of the Kruger National Park
– Leo Braack
Field Guide to the Snakes and other Reptiles of Southern Africa
– Bill Branch

Reptiles

Reptiles are cold-blooded and need to absorb energy from the sun. During the winter months they are easy to spot, warming themselves on exposed rocks, tree trunks or sand banks.

Throughout the Park

A	E	I	M
B	F	J	N
C	G	K	O
D	H	L	P

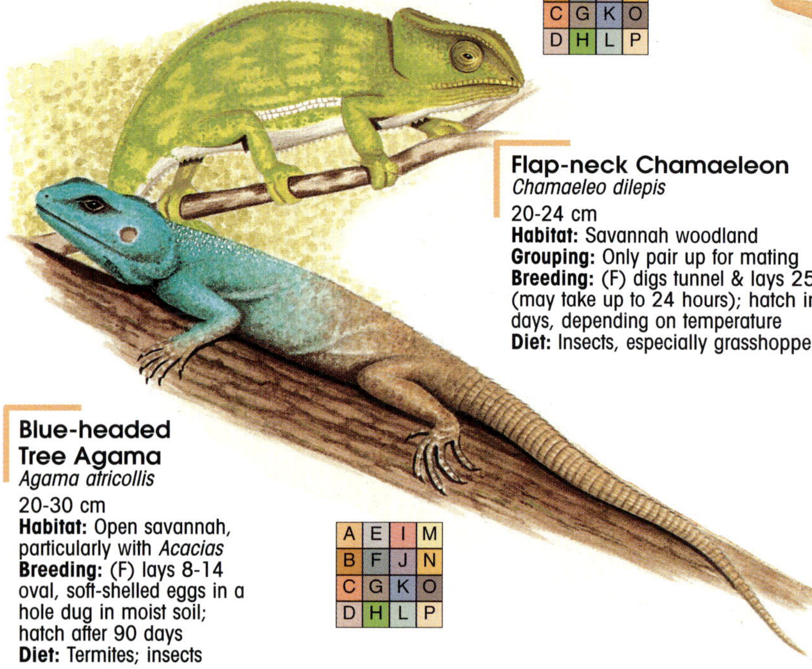

Flap-neck Chamaeleon
Chamaeleo dilepis
20-24 cm
Habitat: Savannah woodland
Grouping: Only pair up for mating
Breeding: (F) digs tunnel & lays 25-50 eggs (may take up to 24 hours); hatch in 150-300 days, depending on temperature
Diet: Insects, especially grasshoppers & beetles

Blue-headed Tree Agama
Agama atricollis
20-30 cm
Habitat: Open savannah, particularly with *Acacias*
Breeding: (F) lays 8-14 oval, soft-shelled eggs in a hole dug in moist soil; hatch after 90 days
Diet: Termites; insects

A	E	I	M
B	F	J	N
C	G	K	O
D	H	L	P

Nile Crocodile
Crocodylus niloticus
2,5-3,5 m; 70-100 kg
(may exceed 1000 kg)
Grouping: Communal
Breeding: 16-18 eggs are laid in nest-site in sunny bank; defended by (F); after they hatch young carried to the water in her mouth; attentive parents
Diet: Fish; antelope; carrion

A	E	I	M
B	F	J	N
C	G	K	O
D	H	L	P

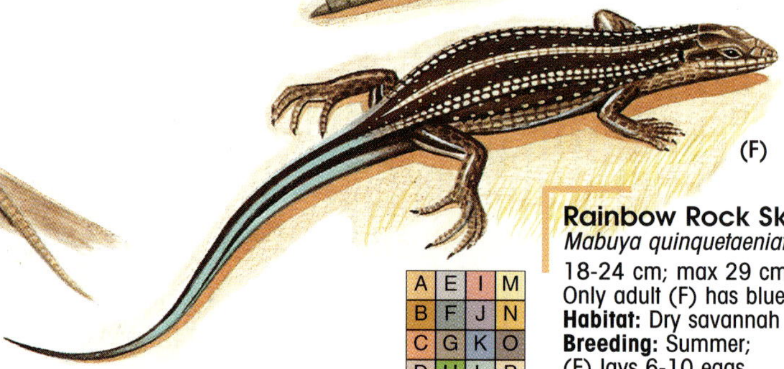

(F)

Rainbow Rock Skink
Mabuya quinquetaeniata
18-24 cm; max 29 cm
Only adult (F) has blue tail
Habitat: Dry savannah
Breeding: Summer; (F) lays 6-10 eggs
Diet: Mainly insects

A	E	I	M
B	F	J	N
C	G	K	O
D	H	L	P

African Rock Python
Python sebae natalensis
3-5 m; max 5,6 m
Habitat: Woodland, often near permanent water
Breeding: Lay 30-50 eggs in disused burrows; protected by (F); hatch in 65-80 days
Diet: Small antelope; monkeys; fish; ground roosting birds; rodents; (kill by constricting prey)

A	E	I	M
B	F	J	N
C	G	K	O
D	H	L	P

Always near water

A	E	I	M
B	F	J	N
C	G	K	O
D	H	L	P

Leguaan (Nile/Water Monitor)
Varanus niloticus
1,0-1,4 m; max 2,1 m
Largest African lizard; excellent swimmer
Habitat: In vegetation alongside larger rivers & dams
Grouping: May hibernate communally
Breeding: Aug – Sep, after first rains; (F) lays 20-60 eggs in active termite nest; incubated at constant temperature & humidity; may take 1 year to hatch
Diet: Crabs; mussels; fish; frogs; birds; eggs; insects

Leguaan (Rock Monitor)
Varanus exanthematicus
More heavily built than the Nile/Water monitor; thicker head; blunter nose
0,7-1,0 m; max 1,3 m
Habitat: Dry savannah; trunks, holes & disused animal burrows
Grouping: Usually solitary; hibernates
Breeding: Aug – Sep; (F) may lay 8-37 eggs in active termite nest; otherwise in hole in moist soil; take 1 year to hatch
Diet: Millipedes; beetles; grasshoppers; carrion; baby tortoises

A	E	I	M
B	F	J	N
C	G	K	O
D	H	L	P

Mike Parkin

Insects

Insects are the biggest group of all creatures in Kruger. They are essential to the maintenance of the balance in the ecosystem. They return food material directly into the soil and they play a vital role in pollinating plants. They are on average the most colourful of all Kruger's wildlife! Look out for them around the camp fires at night, and in trees during the day.

Always near water

Dragonfly
Odonata

Different varieties with wingspans 4,5-14 cm
Habitat: Large rivers & dams
Breeding: (F) lays eggs while skimming the water; eggs drift to the bottom & young (nymphs) hatch after a few days; nymphs propel themselves forward by sucking in water & squirting it out
Diet: Adults & nymphs feed on insects

A	E	I	M
B	F	J	N
C	G	K	O
D	H	L	P

Koppie Charaxes
Charaxes jasius saturnus

Over 200 species of butterfly are seen regularly; charaxes are particularly spectacular, with tail-like extensions on their hind-wings
Diet: Can often be seen sucking fluid from elephant dung or the sap of damaged trees

A	E	I	M
B	F	J	N
C	G	K	O
D	H	L	P

Honeybee
Apis mellifera adansonii

A	E	I	M
B	F	J	N
C	G	K	O
D	H	L	P

Very important insects as they make honey and pollinate plants
Habitat: Widespread with hives often in rock crevices
Grouping: Well-ordered social communities
Breeding: Each hive has one queen, which mates with (M) bees (drones), and lays thousands of eggs a day in summer
Diet: Nectar; pollen

Mopane Eemperor Moth & Worm
Gonimbrasia belina

Have large "eye" spots on wings; adult moths are nocturnal
Habitat: Caterpillars are found only in summer in Mopane trees
Utilization: A delicacy for birds & man

A	E	I	M
B	F	J	N
C	G	K	O
D	H	L	P

Throughout the Park

Cicada (Christmas Beetle)
Cicadidae

20 mm
Found throughout Kruger; seldom seen,
because of their perfect camouflage; singing in summer is a characteristic sound of Lowveld bush; sound made by leg muscles vibrating against a special membrane
Breeding: Adults live for only a few weeks – to find a mate, copulate & lay eggs; nymphs that hatch from the eggs live underground for many years before emerging

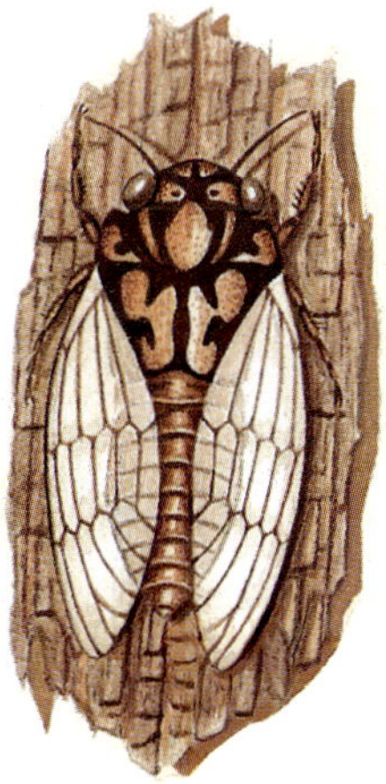

A	E	I	M
B	F	J	N
C	G	K	O
D	H	L	P

Locust
Orthoptera

Many are cryptically coloured to hide them in vegetation
Habitat: Wide variety
Grouping: Red locust can form huge swarms on northern plains
Breeding: Eggs are normally laid in a hole in the soil
Diet: Vegetation
Utilization: Important source of food for mammals, birds & lizards

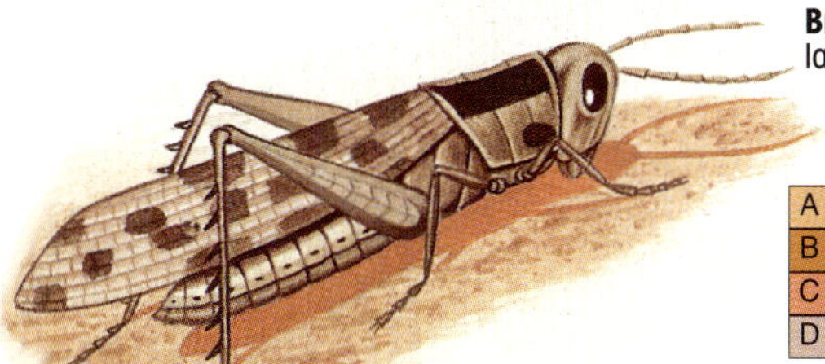

A	E	I	M
B	F	J	N
C	G	K	O
D	H	L	P

Termite (White Ant/Flying Ant)
Macrotermes michaelsenii

Habitat: Live in huge termitaria (anthills); structure of the termitaria regulates both temperature & humidity conditions perfectly
Utilization: Important food source for aardvark & birds

A	E	I	M
B	F	J	N
C	G	K	O
D	H	L	P

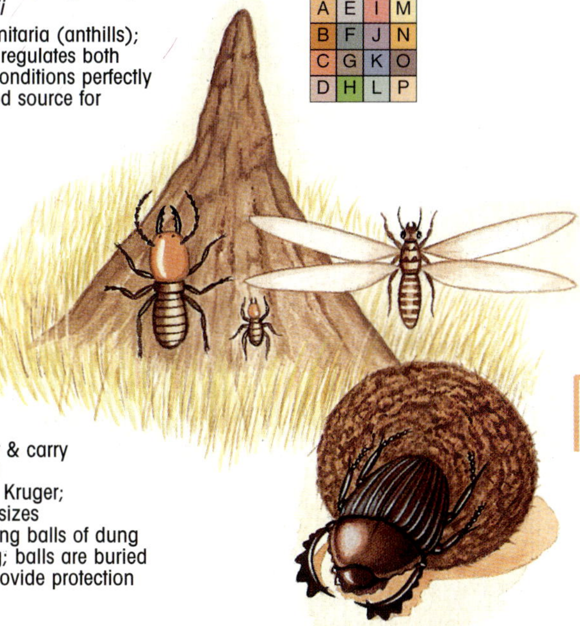

A	E	I	M
B	F	J	N
C	G	K	O
D	H	L	P

Anopheles Mosquito
Anophelinae

Only (F) carries malaria; common throughout Kruger from Oct – May
Habitat: Abundant mainly along rivers, streams, pans & waterholes; malaria mosquitoes breed in shallow rain pools & therefore occur everywhere
Breeding: Lay eggs in standing water
Diet: (M) feeds on juice of rotting fruit; (F) sucks blood; feed (bite) actively, from dusk to dawn

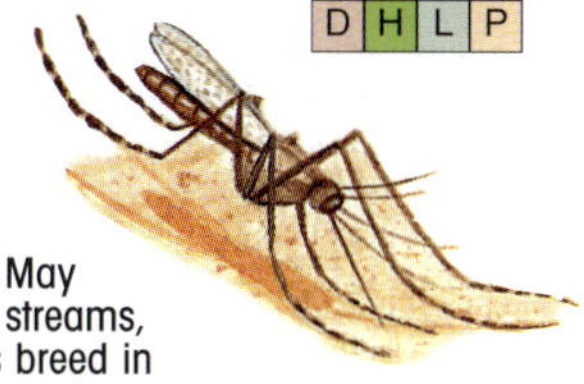

A	E	I	M
B	F	J	N
C	G	K	O
D	H	L	P

Dung Beetle
Scarabaeinae

50 mm
Clean up decaying matter & carry the nutrients underground
Habitat: Very common in Kruger; many species of different sizes
Breeding: Often seen rolling balls of dung in which they lay one egg; balls are buried to maintain moisture & provide protection against predators

A	E	I	M
B	F	J	N
C	G	K	O
D	H	L	P

Antlion
Myrmeleonidae

12 mm
Adults resemble dragonflies; mostly nocturnal
Habitat: Conical pits in sandy areas, often seen at picnic sites
Diet: Larvae prey on ants & other crawling insects which slip down & are trapped in the sandy pit

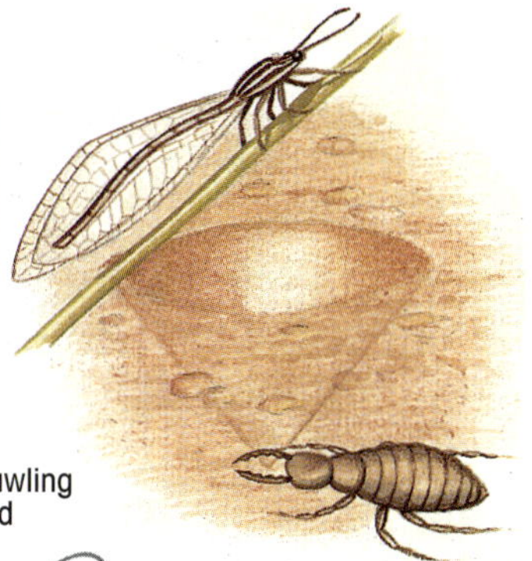

Mike Parkin

Other small creatures

Throughout the Park

A	E	I	M
B	F	J	N
C	G	K	O
D	H	L	P

Community Spider
Stegodyphus dumicola

Very small
Grouping: Live socially
Breeding: For protection they make large bird-like nests, with many spiders in one nest
Diet: Threads spun around the nest catch prey, which is shared by all occupants of nest
Utilization: Web used by some birds in their nest building

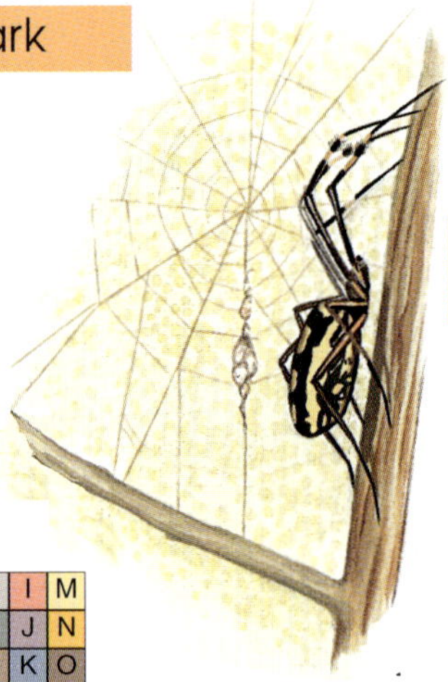

A	E	I	M
B	F	J	N
C	G	K	O
D	H	L	P

Golden Orbweb Spider
Nephila senegalensis

25-30 mm
Large spider; spectacular, golden, orb-shaped webs, seen early in the morning laden with dew
Diet: Insects, captured in web

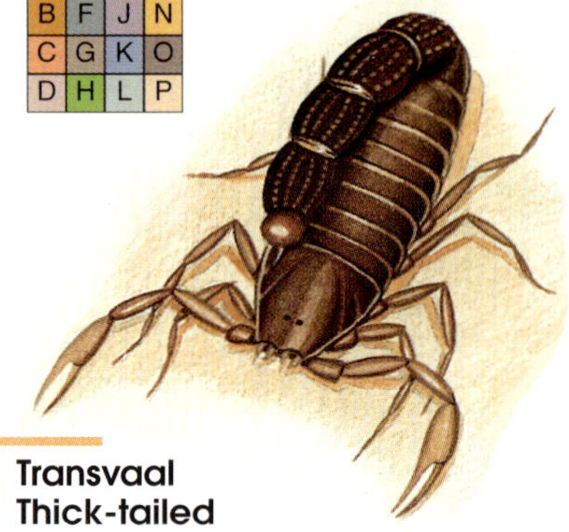

A	E	I	M
B	F	J	N
C	G	K	O
D	H	L	P

Transvaal Thick-tailed Scorpion
Parabuthus transvaalicus

Up to 14 cm
Related to spiders; stings can be dangerous to humans; thick tail, small pinchers
Habitat: Under stones; in burrows & dead logs
Diet: Insects; spiders; small lizards; other scorpions

Millipede (Songololo)
Diplopoda

Up to 20 cm
Some varieties defend themselves with poisonous fluid (containing hydrogen cyanide) from headglands; roll into a ball when disturbed
Habitat: Usually found in moist places
Diet: Plant-eating, preferring rotten leaves

A	E	I	M
B	F	J	N
C	G	K	O
D	H	L	P

Giant Land Snail
Achatina

13-20 cm
Can be seen in the early morning after rain; usually nocturnal; can live up to 10 years
Breeding: Lay up to 500 eggs annually
Diet: Omnivorous, eating dead animals & plants

A	E	I	M
B	F	J	N
C	G	K	O
D	H	L	P

A	E	I	M
B	F	J	N
C	G	K	O
D	H	L	P

Leopard Tortoise
Geochelone pardalis babcocki

30-45 cm, max 72 cm; 8-12 kg
Breeding: Mating (at 15 years old) is fairly robust, with the (M) pushing & butting the (F) into submission; 6-15 eggs are laid in a hole in the ground
Diet: Wide variety of plants; fruit

Always near water

A	E	I	M
B	F	J	N
C	G	K	O
D	H	L	P

Olive Toad
Bufo garmani

3-5 cm
Habitat: On land in damp places
Diet: Insects, especially termites & moths; nocturnal hunters

Serrated Hinged Terrapin
Pelusios sinuatus

30-40 cm
Habitat: Often seen basking on rocks & logs during the day
Diet: Carrion; mussels; invertebrates; frogs; even take ticks off the legs of buffalo drinking water

A	E	I	M
B	F	J	N
C	G	K	O
D	H	L	P

Foam Nest Frog
Chiromantis xerampelina

7-8 cm
Habitat: Tree branches overhanging water
Breeding: Eggs mixed into a foam nest; tadpoles hatch here & drop into water
Diet: Tadpoles feed on algae & decaying vegetation

A	E	I	M
B	F	J	N
C	G	K	O
D	H	L	P

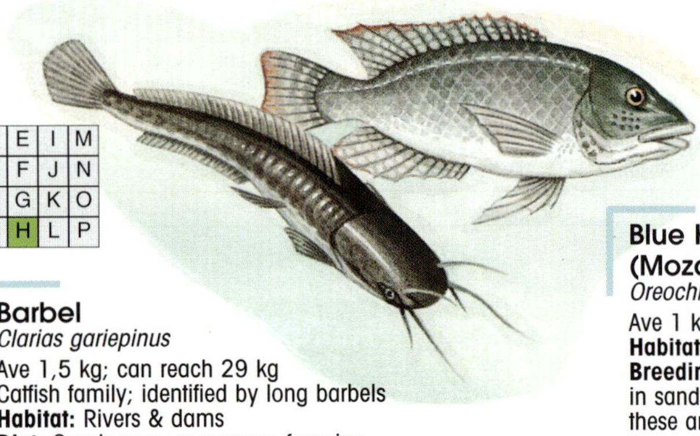

A	E	I	M
B	F	J	N
C	G	K	O
D	H	L	P

Barbel
Clarias gariepinus

Ave 1,5 kg; can reach 29 kg
Catfish family; identified by long barbels
Habitat: Rivers & dams
Diet: Omnivorous scavenger, foraging mostly at night
Utilization: Important in the diet of crocodiles

A	E	I	M
B	F	J	N
C	G	K	O
D	H	L	P

Blue Kurper (Mozambique Tilapia)
Oreochromis mossambicus

Ave 1 kg
Habitat: Slow-flowing rivers
Breeding: (M) scoops a depression in sandbed of pool for (F) to lay eggs; these are sucked into her mouth where they are kept until hatching
Diet: Omnivorous

ılamela Iron Age site, see page 41

Restoration of ancient sites is ongoing in the Kruger National Park.

Paul Kruger monument at Paul Kruger Gate, see page 42

The Stevenson-Hamilton Library in Skukuza houses fascinating historical records of the Park, see page 42

HISTORY

Everything in Nature is linked

The first part of this book shows how geology, plants and animals depend on one another for healthy survival. The following pages outline the history of humans in the Lowveld, from the earliest inhabitants, to the establishment of Kruger as a National Park.

Ancient artifacts have been uncovered in this area indicating the presence of humans for thousands of years.

Technological advancements over the past 200 years have helped humans to achieve safer and more comfortable lives.

However the planet's environment has paid a heavy price for man's development. It is important to remember that wherever we live, whatever our life style and environment, everything around us is linked back to Earth.

This link must be maintained at all costs. As you travel home, remember how important every link in the chain is... and at home, you too can play an important role to keep these links healthy and viable.

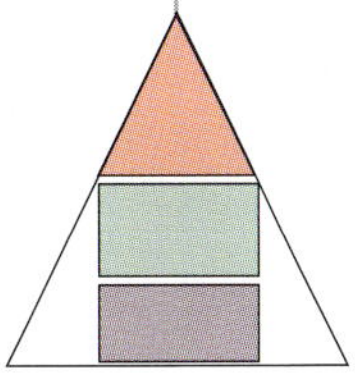

EVERYTHING IN NATURE IS LINKED

Read your Entry/Exit permit for more information on the Park rules.

HISTORY

Over thousands of years people have lived in what is today the Kruger National Park. They did not change the environment very much and so today we can imagine what life must have been like here for human beings in the distant past. At first it must have been a short and brutish existence, but as time went by, humans began to conquer nature, and survival in this wild place became easier. Our relationship with nature has developed from one of co-existence to one of destruction and abuse, and finally to conservation. Today we face the challenges of the present to determine the future, but we do this with the knowledge of the past ...

32 The numbers in this section correspond with the numbered icons on the KNP Map, as well as with those summarised on the small history map on page 43.

The numbers on both Maps follow numerical sequence (1-75), from the north to the south.

I STONE AGE

Stones and bones

Archaeologists have discovered that early humans roamed through the Lowveld as far back as one and a half million years ago. These ancient humans *(Homo erectus)* left clues for us about their prehistoric lives, such as stone tools, their skeletons and the bones of the animals they ate. From this evidence we can get some idea of how they lived and what they looked like.

The average brain size of *Homo erectus* was 935 cubic centimetres, compared with modern people's 1 345 cubic centimetres. Heaps of bones that have been found of now extinct animals, like the mammoth, the short-necked giraffe and the oversized baboon, show they hunted, but they mainly scavenged and foraged for food. Stone tools from this time have been found at the confluences of the Luvuvhu and Limpopo, as well as the Letaba and Olifants Rivers. This is proof that they were 'human', because their actions were planned and their artifacts were designed for specific purposes. But early humans had to adapt to, and move with, a changing climate. Sometimes dwelling sites were evacuated for thousands of years as the people moved off to find better game and a favourable climate.

During the Middle Stone Age (100 000-40 000 BC) humans gradually became more refined. Today we find ourselves in the 'space age', but the human capacity for invention began a long, long time ago.

San hunter-gatherer

The San – inventors and artists

The Late Stone Age began 40 000 years ago. "Necessity is the mother of invention", and in order to survive, *Homo sapiens* learnt to develop more efficient tools and weapons. Small bands of nomadic hunter-gatherers, known as the San, lived and moved through the Lowveld. There were giant leaps in technology with advances like fishing hooks, tools for gathering food, and the bow and arrow (developed about 10 000 years ago). Poisoned arrows made hunting easier. They were made from the poison bush, certain *Euphorbia* trees, poison rope, and the venom of snakes and spiders. These developments gave the San time to refine their tools and weapons even more – and it gave them time to paint.

On a rock face at Renosterkoppies, there is a painting that dates back thousands of years. It is one of about 150 San engraving and painting sites found so far in Kruger. These paintings were central to the San's rituals and religion and give us a glimpse of their spiritual beliefs and practices, and their dances and trances which healed the sick and connected them with the spirit world. The paintings also depict nature which for them was both earthly and divine.

It is thought that the San used egg white, animal fat and blood as binding agents for coloured pigments. Hair from the manes and tails of animals was carefully made into the first paint brushes. They also used feathers and their fingers to record glimpses of life in the Stone Age. (site 56 on the Wolhuter Trail, and site 63).

II IRON AGE

The first farmers

For centuries the San lived without competition for resources. But as early as 200 AD, more technologically advanced people, the Bantu-speaking farmers, immigrated into the Lowveld and settled along the banks of the Limpopo, Luvuvhu, Shingwedzi, Letaba and later the Sabie and Crocodile Rivers. They brought crops and herds of domestic animals and the secret of metal-work. This was the beginning of the Iron Age in southern Africa.

Archaeologists have discovered that for hundreds of years this new civilisation lived alongside the San, sharing the abundance provided by the bush. As more people moved into the area, the San were gradually pushed out, although scattered groups still inhabited the area as late as the 19th century.

The new farmers were still dependant on their environment. There is evidence that, between 800-1600 AD, the area suffered poor farming conditions, game became scarcer, and many groups moved off to better pastures. Those who stayed relied on hunting and trade.

Fingerprinting the past

In Kruger archaeologists have identified different periods by the different types of pottery that were made. So far more than 12 different cultural groups have been identified, some dating back to 200 AD. Each form of pottery is like a fingerprint of a different time and group of people. Beautiful 'fluted' clay vessels have been found near Mopane Camp and at Silver Leaves, close to Tzaneen. This is the earliest archaeological record of the early farmers in South Africa. These vessels show the fine craftsmanship of the first black settler farmers as far back as the second century AD.

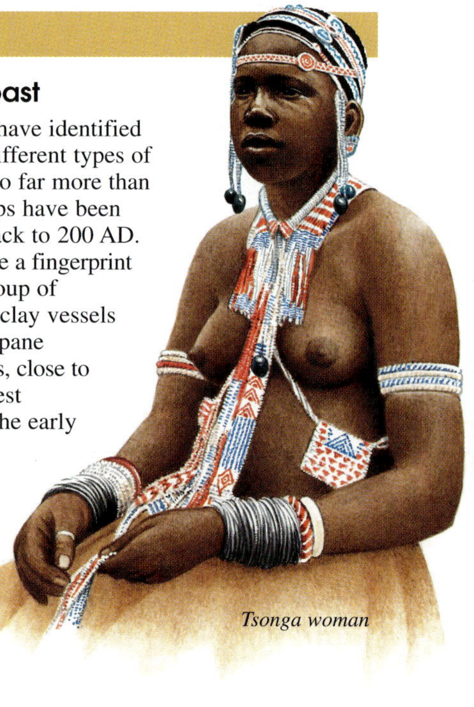

Tsonga woman

Early trade – black, white and yellow gold

International trade in South Africa began about 1 000 years before gold was discovered on the Witwatersrand. Copper from Phalaborwa and Balule (site 21), salt from Eiland, and crops like sorghum and beans, had long been traded locally. But the Lowveld and the interior had far more exotic goods that attracted the attention of Arab traders in search of riches and new products. Africa had 'white gold', in the form of elephant ivory. It had yellow gold, the precious metal that kings and sultans desired. And in the Late Iron Age, it had 'black gold' – the slaves.

The interest from Arab traders in the 9th and 10th centuries, resulted in the rise of the Mapungubwe kingdom, based at the confluence of the Limpopo and Shashe Rivers (current Zimbabwe / Botswana border). Trade goods were brought from Arab seaports on the east coast, like Sofala. This affected people living in and around today's Kruger National Park, who soon formed states allied to Mapungubwe, at places like Makahane and Shilowa (1000-1300 AD).

After 1200 AD Great Zimbabwe succeeded Mapungubwe as the inland trade capital. In the Lowveld, stone-built royal dwellings were constructed at Thulamela, Matekevhele and other sites (visit Thulamela by appointment – site 11). Dzundzwini, (site 9) meaning 'the fields that belong to the chief and the people' provided food to traders and visitors to the royal enclosure. Another interesting historical name from this period is Gumbandebuu, which means 'the shearing of the beards' and refers to the Venda initiation school that led young men symbolically and religiously into adulthood.

Masorini Stone Age Site

These chiefdoms left testimony to a profitable international trade – glass beads, Chinese porcelain, home-woven and imported cloth, ivory bracelets, gold, bronze, copper and iron artifacts and jewellery. Much of the iron produced was traded with the agriculturally rich areas of the eastern escarpment.

Masorini, once also a Stone Age site, was still a powerful centre for the production of iron tools and weapons in the 19th century. Standing at this prehistoric site (site 19), one is struck by the power of images from thousands of years ago. In the words of Prof. Hannes Eloff, *"it is as if the actors have left the stage, but the set remains intact"*.

III EUROPEAN EXPLORERS

White man's grave

It wasn't until 1725 that the first European encountered the hostile Lowveld. Francois de Cuiper, a Dutchman, crossed the Lebombo Mountains. No sooner had he entered the present day Kruger National Park, than he was attacked at Gomondwane (site 61) and beat a hasty retreat to the coast. For another century the area remained a mystery to adventurous Europeans, who had already circumnavigated the world but had not yet conquered or colonised Africa or its people. In time the Lowveld became known as 'the white man's grave'.

The first European to return was João Albasini, a Portuguese trader who ventured from Delagoa Bay (Maputo) in 1830, and began establishing tradelinks inland. Albasini's larger than life personality, his willingness to learn local language, and the help of the warrior chiefs Manungu and Jozikhulu, enabled him to survive. People living along the Sabie River felt they were under his protection and in turn protected him (sites 33, 51, 58).

By this time, the Voortrekker people had settled in the Transvaal. It became imperative, if they were to escape the fetters of the British Empire, that they discover the ancient African trade routes to the east coast. Lang Hans van Rensberg and his small group left Zoutpansberg in 1836 . They were never seen again. His compatriot, Louis Trichardt, set out to find him and to open the route to Delagoa Bay. João Albasini was there to meet the survivors of the gruelling trek. Trichardt, his wife and most of his people, died of malaria. (sites relating to this period are 6, 15, 26, 50, 57, 60; other trade sites are 64, 65, 67, 69, 73).

Albasini ruins

Golden years – prospectors, crooks and hunters

In 1873, gold was discovered in the Lowveld. Hordes of fortune-seeking prospectors flooded in. More than ever, it was necessary to establish links with the east coast in order to get food and machinery for the miners. (sites 12, 48). A Hungarian man, Alois Nellmapius, was contracted to build the road to Delagoa Bay. Sir Percy FitzPatrick used this route for his transport riders. Memorials to FitzPatrick's famous Staffordshire terrier, Jock, can be seen at sites 49, 68, 71.

At the same time, the Lowveld attracted many criminals and hunters (sites 13, 74). Colourful characters, like Bvekenya Barnard of Ivory Trail fame, made their living from selling ivory, both legally and illegally. Those escaping the law headed for "Crooks' Corner" (site 3), which borders on three countries – South Africa, Moçambique and Zimbabwe. From here they only needed to hop across one of three borders to safety. (other sites are 1, 8)

Jock of the Bushveld memorial

'A mad and delightful mania'

The free and romantic lifestyle attracted fearless and eccentric characters, like Barnard and William Cornwallis-Harris. The latter said of himself that he found hunting *"a truly most delightful mania."* As time went by, many hunters realised they could not survive off ivory trade alone. They turned from the white gold of ivory to the black gold of recruiting labour for the Witwatersrand mines.

Cheap labour, WNLA and the pass laws

"In the midst of trouble and sorrow we left our children at home, children full of tears, crying tears; ... father is gone, is gone; God, help fathers to return." (From ***Another Blanket***. Agency of Industrial Mission). These words were sung by prospective recruitments for the Witwatersrand gold mines at the turn of the century.

For some years, labour was illegally traded from the present day Kruger, but later only the Witwatersrand Native Labour Association was allowed to recruit (sites 4, 5). Once in Johannesburg, the labourers lived in appalling conditions, but migrant labour continued to be the mainstay of South Africa's mining industry.

IV THE BEGINNING OF KRUGER

The first reserve and forced removals

By the end of the century, hunting mania had wiped out the Lowveld's huge herds of game. In 1898, President Paul Kruger proclaimed the area between the Crocodile and Sabie Rivers as the Sabie Reserve. This was fortunate timing as for the next 4 years, politicians, hunters and fortune-seekers were too busy fighting the Anglo-Boer war to care about conservation (site 66).

After the war the British victors reproclaimed the Reserve (site 20 relates to this period). They set about clearing the way for the protected area. This involved the forced removal of local inhabitants and in 1903, between 2 000-3 000 people were moved out of the Sabie Reserve. Similar removals were conducted throughout Kruger's history. In 1969, after many years of dispute, the Makuleke people were moved out of the Pafuri area. Land claims today continue the dispute between the need to conserve a natural heritage, and the people's need for both land and work.

He who turns things upside down

Major James Stevenson-Hamilton was appointed the first warden and told to manage a piece of land the size of the Netherlands. The short statured, short tempered Scotsman achieved this and earned himself the name 'Skukuza', meaning he who turns things upside down. Stevenson waged war on poaching and managed to persuade the government to expand the Reserve to include the whole area between the Crocodile and Luvuvhu Rivers. Farmers voiced stiff opposition, accusing the Reserve of being "a breeding ground for lions". Both domestic stock and people were often attacked, as men like Harry Wolhuter could testify. Possibly South Africa's most famous ranger, he was attacked by lions in 1903. As the big male dragged him off, he felt for its heart and stabbed it fatally with his pocket knife (site 27).

Living in solitude, far from any form of civilisation, rangers like Wolhuter, Gaza Gray, Helfas Nkuna, Jafuta Shithlave, Njinja Ndlovu and G.R. Healy laid the foundations for the Kruger National Park. Today we still enjoy the benefits of their energy and vision (sites 29, 32, 34, 35, 37, 55).

A train reaction

A deciding factor in the creation of the Kruger National Park, was the Eastern and Selati railway lines (relevant sites are 44, 45, 47, 62). By the time the lines were completed in 1912, very little gold was being mined in the Selati gold fields. In order to make the railway profitable, a 9 day tour of the Lowveld and Moçambique was started. The most popular part of the tour proved to be the game viewing and a night under the stars at present day Skukuza. The fact that people would pay to see game, not just to shoot it, gave Stevenson-Hamilton the support he needed to proclaim the Reserve a National Park.

Word, deed and law

If Paul Kruger had spoken the first word regarding the protection of the Lowveld's wildlife, and James Stevenson-Hamilton had been the first to physically protect it, then Piet Grobler, Minister of Lands in 1926, takes the credit for legalising the reserve as a National Park (site 22). He successfully passed the Bill on National Parks through the government and named the area Kruger National Park. Private landowners, like Eileen Orpen (sites 23, 30), with a love of wildlife, donated land to the Park, increasing its size. The protection of all wildlife within the Park, and the development of tourism, were now official policy and the road forward was clear.

In 1927 three cars entered the Park. Two years later there were 850 cars. And over the next 50 years some 150 000 people visited the Kruger National Park annually. Today there are 700 000 wildlife enthusiasts who visit every year, enjoying the fruits of a long, fascinating and hard-won battle to create one of the finest Game Parks in the world.
(The following sites refer to development of Kruger, but do not appear in the text 2, 7, 10, 14, 16-18, 24, 25, 28, 31, 36, 38-43, 46, 52-54, 59, 70, 72, 75).

Further reading:
Neem uit die verlede – Dr U de V Pienaar
South African Eden – James Stevenson-Hamilton

Stevenson-Hamilton memorial

Historical sites

The colours used on this page tie up with the colours of the headings on pages 40-42. These historical sites are also marked in the same way on the KNP Map, with this icon.

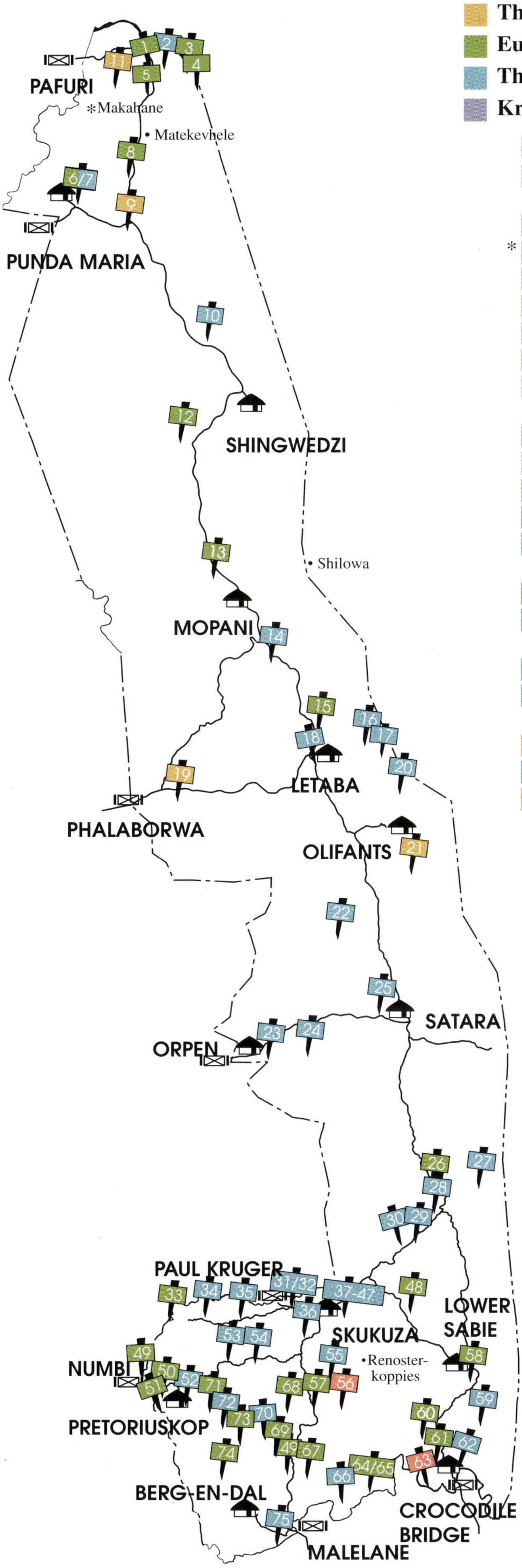

The Stone Age

The Iron Age

European Explorers

The Beginning of Kruger

Kruger today – see page 44

- 1 Bobomeni Drift
- 2 Old Pafuri tented camp site (at picnic site)
- 3 "Crooks' Corner"
- * 4 WNLA recruiting station
- 5 Baobab Hill
- 6 Potgieter's route
- 7 Donations acknowledged
- 8 Klopperfontein Drift
- 9 Dzundwini Spring (also Ranger J.J. Coetzer's quarters)
- 10 Early bore-hole
- 11 Thulamela Iron Age site
- 12 Red Rocks
- 13 Bowker Kop
- 14 Old Shawu picnic site (Mooi Plaas)
- 15 Das Neves' cross
- 16 Anna Ledeboer's grave – ranger's wife
- 17 Engelhard plaque (Dam)
- 18 Ranger L.H. Ledeboer's quarters
- 19 Masorini historical site
- 20 Von Wielligh's baobab
- 21 Balule (Reitz's pontoon)
- 22 Grobler plaque (Dam)
- 23 Orpen memorial (Orpen)
- 24 Original hut at Rabelais' entrance gate (small museum)
- * 25 William Lloyd's grave
- 26 Trichardt's memorial
- 27 Ranger Harry Wolhuter's lion attack plaque
- 28 Sausage tree where ranger G.C.S. Crous erected his "wattle-and-daub" quarters (at Tshokwane)
- 29 Kruger memorial tablets
- 30 Orpen memorial koppie
- 31 Acknowledgement to rangers (Paul Kruger Gate)
- 32 Paul Kruger monument (Paul Kruger Gate)
- 33 Albasini Ruins/ information display
- 34 Wolhuter's camp "Doispane"
- 35 Wolhuter's outspan (Spanplek)
- 36 De Laporte's windmill

*Sites not accessible to visitors at time of print

- 37 Stevenson-Hamilton memorial library & information centre
- 38 Board member W.A. Campbell hut/museum
- 39 Pet cemetery (Skukuza)
- 40 Struben cottage (Skukuza)
- 41 Papenfus' clock tower (Skukuza)
- 42 Memorial to honour the founders of KNP
- 43 Pontoon crossing
- 44 Selati line and rail bridge
- 45 Selati train restaurant and museum (Skukuza)
- 46 First bore-hole (Skukuza)
- 47 Huhla siding (Skukuza)
- 48 Prospectors' graves
- 49 Jock of the Bushveld's plaque
- 50 Pretorius' grave
- * 51 Manungu's kraal
- 52 "Wattle-and-daub" hut, built for tourists 1930 (Pretoriuskop)
- 53 Wolhuter's windmill
- 54 Board member Joe Ludorf plaque (Napi Kop)
- 55 Stevenson-Hamilton memorial & "grave" (Shirimantanga Koppie)
- 56 Bushman paintings (Wolhuter Trail)
- 57 Old Delagoa – Lydenburg wagon road
- 58 Albasini's trading post (Lower Sabie)
- 59 Duke's windmill
- 60 Sardelli's store
- 61 Francois de Cuiper's attack
- 62 Crocodile River railway bridge
- 63 Bushman paintings (Crocodile Bridge hippo pool)
- 64 Old trade route
- 65 Alf Roberts' trading store
- 66 General Ben Viljoen's attack site
- 67 Outspan plaques
- 68 Jock of the Bushveld & Sable statue (Jock camp)
- 69 Outspan plaque
- 70 First concrete dam (Ntomeni Spruit)
- 71 Jock of the Bushveld's birth place
- 72 Early bore-hole (Komapiti)
- 73 Thomas Hart's grave
- 74 Stols Nek (on Wolhuter Trail)
- 75 Harold Trollope hut (Malelane)

Most animals in Kruger do not run away as a motor car approaches because they are used to vehicles. However this does not mean that they are tame. In fact they are wild, and when afraid they can become extremely dangerous. Many of them are afraid of humans – and if you leave the safety of your car, your life can be in danger. **Only** get out of your vehicle in rest camps and at places marked on the Maps as **Get-out points** . Places marked as are **Look-out Points** where you must stay in your vehicle.

Lions roam freely – stay in your vehicle!

Gate times

Unless indicated, these times are for both **Entry** and **Camp** gates.

	Jan	Feb	Mar	Apr	May-Jul	Aug	Sept	Oct	Nov-Dec
Open	04:30 (camp gate) 05:30 (entry gate)	05:30	05:30	06:00	06:00	06:00	06:00	05:30	04:30 (camp gate) 05:30 (entry gate)
Close	18:30	18:30	18:00	18:00	17:30	18:00	18:00	18:00	18:30

Planning your drive

Plan your drives carefully. There are no petrol stations and few rest rooms, toilets or shops between camps. Before you set off...

Be sure you have the following inside the car:

- ❐ an up-to-date map
- ❐ enough to eat and drink
- ❐ cameras, film, binoculars, reference books
- ❐ litter bag

Get-out points, like picnic sites, are marked on the Maps.

Food for thought

Nature provides the perfect diet for all living creatures. By feeding animals we disturb the natural chain and the animal and its young are discouraged from finding their own food. Human's food also causes digestive disorders in animals. Feeding monkeys and baboons can be dangerous to you, as well as endanger their lives. Once they become a nuisance or a threat to humans, they have to be shot by rangers.

Take a break

It is a good idea to stop often, if possible near a game path or a waterhole, even if there is nothing obvious to see. If you switch your engine and air conditioner off, and wait quietly, you will almost always be rewarded. It is safest to stop quite a distance away from elephants with young, particularly if your engine is turned off. Elephant cows can be very aggressive when separated from their young by a vehicle.

Sunset over the Lowveld